Historic Tales of the PENNSYLVANIA Wilds

Kathy Myers

Published by The History Press
Charleston, SC
www.historypress.com

Front cover: (*Top*) *Sinnemahoning Creek. Courtesy of Nicholas A., www.Tonelli@flickr.com.* (*Bottom*) *Two Bull Elk Sparring During the Annual Fall Mating Ritual Known as the "Rut." Courtesy of Paul Staniszewski.*

First published 2021

Manufactured in the United States

ISBN 9781467149204

Library of Congress Control Number: 2021931240

Notice: The information in this book is true and complete to the best of our knowledge. It is offered without guarantee on the part of the author or The History Press. The author and The History Press disclaim all liability in connection with the use of this book.

To the men in my life:

My husband, John, who was my high school sweetheart and who has remained my sweetheart as we have walked together through life's adventures.

My son, Andrew, my only child, who has been a blessing to me from his first day and from whom I have gained an appreciation for the history of this region.

My two grandsons, Henry and John, from their "Granny,"
I have loved every minute of knowing you.

Generations come, and generations go, but the earth lasts forever.
Ecclesiastes 1:4

Contents

Preface

Although I have written articles, annual reports and advertising copy, this is my first book project. Faced with creating a preface, I questioned what goes into writing one. The answer I found is that a preface is to provide an introduction to a book written by the author to inform a potential reader how the book came into being and why they might want to read it. As the author of this work, I offer the following:

What do I know about the early history of the Pennsylvania Wilds? Through a three-year study of one of my family lines, I learned of events that directly affected them and many others who were living on the Pennsylvania frontier—a worldwide conflict known in Europe as the Seven Years' War and in America as the French and Indian War.

If your experience in school was similar to mine, you may recall that the study of the French and Indian War was not extensive; it was barely a footnote in the history of our commonwealth. As I researched, I realized that war was the starting point of understanding what my family and others experienced during those early years. Those events that eventually led our ancestors to fight the most powerful country in the world, Great Britain, in the American Revolution.

My research gave me an understanding of the Delaware Indians who were, at that time, the primary tribe in Pennsylvania. Indian paths and place names jumped out at me from the pages of books I read as part of my research, and I learned about their religion. The story of the Creator and the creation was the basis for their respect for the land and animals, which they believed belonged to us all. Their societal structure was based on kinship, each knowing their place in various clans. Sadly, my research led me to consider that, many times, they were on the losing side of history. In the book's conclusion, I offer a series of "what ifs."

Examining the years between 1755 and 1830, this book is an account of events and people who lived at this time, many eventually settling the region known as the Pennsylvania Wilds. In addition to the early history of Pennsylvania, this book offers vignettes and folklore collected from six counties located in the Wilds: Cameron, Clearfield, Clinton, Elk, Jefferson and Warren.

Acknowledgements

I would like to express many thanks to those who have so willingly supported me throughout this process:

Amayah Pollnac, a ninth-grade student at DuBois Area High School and a longtime student of professional artist Perry Winkler, for her sketches *The Legend of Youngwomanstown* and the *Legend of the Corn*.

Ruth Major, a resident of Martha's Vineyard, Massachusetts, an Arcadia/The History Press coauthor of *Connecticut River Shipbuilding*, and a fine artist, for her portrait of *Shingas, a Delaware Sachem*.

Andrew J. Myers, MA, registered professional archaeologist (RPA), a resident of Kane, Pennsylvania, for the use of his photographs and his research suggestions.

John E. Myers, a resident of Falls Creek, Pennsylvania, and a retired international sales manager for Carlisle/Motion Control, for the use of his photographs and his encouragement.

Paul Staniszewski, a juried Pennsylvania Wilds artisan who taught technology in public schools in northeastern New Jersey. After his retirement, he relocated to north-central Pennsylvania, and he currently resides in Troutville. He shared the use of his beautiful elk photographs with me, and the collection can be found at https://www.shutterstock.com/g/paul+staniszewski or through contacting him directly at paulstan@windstream.net.

Introduction

As I sit at my writing desk in my home on Hemlock Hill, looking out at my personal expanse of forest in the Pennsylvania Wilds, the nation is locked down due to a coronavirus pandemic. Through this troubling time, I find myself reminiscing about the self-reliant and independent spirit of the people who settled this region. What drove them to come into an area that truly was a wilderness, oftentimes leaving behind a refined and settled life? What were their experiences and what was life like for them? What is their lasting legacy? What legends rose up around their experiences? With my family going back twelve generations in this country, I am a part of the seventh generation to reside in the Pennsylvania Wilds. For me, it's simple. The Wilds is my home. Born and raised here, I can't think of another place I'd rather have spent the majority of my life.

As advertised on its webpage:

> *The Pennsylvania Wilds is a special place in America, with fifty state game lands, twenty-nine state parks, nine state and national forests, and sixteen thousand miles of streams and rivers....The Pennsylvania Wilds* [is] *home to seventy percent of our nation's finest headwaters,* [and] *to many people and industries who are able to make their living from the woods...it is also one of the largest expanses of green between New York City and Chicago.*[1]

While the Wilds is composed of twelve and a half counties that cover 25 percent of the state, it is home to only 4 percent of the population of Pennsylvania. These counties include Cameron, Clinton, Clarion, Clearfield, Elk, Forest, Jefferson, Lycoming, McKean, Potter, Tioga, Warren and Northern Centre.[2]

With a rich Indian heritage, place names in Pennsylvania still carry some corrupted version of the original Indian names given by various tribes. A few of the Indian names in the Wilds region that are familiar to many are: Allegheny, Punxsutawney, Mahoning, Kittanning, Sinnemahoning, Lycoming, Tioga, Tionesta, Kinzua, Allegheny, Buckaloon, Catawba, Shawmut, Daguscahonda, Dahoga, Conewango, Toby, Moshannon and Kushequa.[3]

In the following pages, which feature six of the twelve and a half counties in this region, you will find selected vignettes of the history leading up to the settlement of the Wilds, the inhabitants who claimed this region as their home and samples of local folklore. It is my sincere wish that this book will provide you with a great appreciation of this region I call home, the Pennsylvania Wilds.

Part I

The Story Begins

1.
Live Free or Die

A month before the coronavirus outbreak, my husband and I attended a get-together billed as "A Toast to the Winter Edition of *The Watershed Journal*," a quarterly literary magazine produced in the heart of the Pennsylvania Wilds. The event was a celebration of the most-recent edition of the journal, and it gave its writers, including me, an opportunity to present works to the public.

Walking in the front door of the Fusion Café in Brookville, Pennsylvania, that Sunday afternoon, I noticed a couple standing off to one side. Not knowing who they were, my husband and I approached them with friendly conversation. I learned that the gentleman we were speaking to was also one of the writers who was featured in the winter issue of the journal. During the course of our conversation, the couple noted they had recently moved to the area from New Hampshire, remarking positively that they found a similarity between the attitude of the people in the Wilds and that of the people in New Hampshire, an attitude which they described as a "live free or die" spirit. Knowing that famous state motto, I laughed and said, "Yes, we are known for clinging to our guns and Bibles." For me, their comparison of our two groups of people, those in New Hampshire and those in the Pennsylvania Wilds, was a compliment to our way of life.

Where did the motto "live free or die" originate? What spirit does it exemplify? General John Stark, a little-known hero of the Revolutionary War, sent the words in a letter to a group of Patriot veterans of the Battle of Bennington after he was unable to attend their reunion in 1809. He closed his letter by saying, "Live Free or Die: Death is not the worst of Evils." Today, these words are said by some to reflect a spirit of independence that shaped the general's life. To me, these words are stating that death is not the worst of evils if one is forced to live without freedom. General Stark, the writer of those famous words, passed from the scene in 1822, the last surviving general of the American Revolution. The state of New Hampshire adopted "live free or die" as its motto 136 years after the general wrote them.

Many of the settlers of the Pennsylvania Wilds were also Patriots of the American Revolution. Pennsylvania gave its veterans donated lands as a reward for their service in the Pennsylvania Line. Much of the donated land was located in what is known as the Last Purchase of 1784, a final purchase of lands in Pennsylvania from the Native Americans, including the counties that comprise the Pennsylvania Wilds. I suggest that these early settlers were instilled with this same spirit of independence that carried them through the American Revolution to successfully defeat the most powerful country in the world at that time, Great Britain.

It's a spirit that lingers throughout the population of the Pennsylvania Wilds today. Many of the area's modern inhabitants are the descendants of those early settlers. Its citizens are law-abiding people with an independent attitude who are able to take care of their own needs and make and assume responsibility for their decisions.

One historian of the region noted:

> *The pioneers were the self-commissioned explorers and settlers of the New Purchase. Some of them followed the retiring Indians so closely that they cooked their frugal meals by the deserted campfires of the evacuating tribes; others joined the adventurous band in the wilderness, while yet the Allegheny Divide was considered the limit line of settlement, and all may be considered satellites of that star which has carried empire westward since the days of the Revolution. Their objects and hopes belonged to that peculiar form of American civilization which desires, to this day, to settle on the horizon, a feat of irresistible fascination to them, which they performed practically, although the thing was theoretically impossible.*[4]

In this quote, the historian refers to the natural barrier created by the Allegheny Mountains, which run through the Pennsylvania Wilds, and the difficulties settlers had in overcoming this mountainous range. The name Allegheny is Indian in origin.

> *Probably a corruption of Alligewi-hanna, "stream of the Alligewi."… Others give the name a meaning similar to that of Ohio, "fair or beautiful river."…The Alligewi, or more correctly, Talligewi, was a tribe, according to the traditions of the Delaware, once occupying the region east of the Mississippi drained by the Ohio River and its various tributaries.*[5]

Eventually, the name was attached to the chief mountain chain of the Appalachian system. "This range, which is the most lofty and the hardest to cross…and presented the greatest difficulties in the way of all the early traders, road makers and railroad builders."[6] There is an identity that has been attached to people of this region of Pennsylvania. They are known as stump jumpers, as it is said one of their legs is shorter than the other from walking around the sides of the mountains.

The various tribes of Indians over the years established paths through the wilderness. These early paths were the routes by which the first white settlers came into the region—the Shamokin, Chinklacamoose, Kittanning, Catawba, Sinnemahoning and Cornplanter-Venango Paths, to name a few.[7] In many areas, Pennsylvania's modern roadways follow parts of these early Indian paths.

From stargazing in the Wilds to exploring its forests and streams, along the way, the people you meet may very well be the descendants of those early settlers you will encounter in the chapters of this book.

2.
INDIAN PATHS OF PENNSYLVANIA

With the advent of European settlement, the Indian foot trails that laced the Pennsylvania wilderness often became bridle paths, wagon roads, and, eventually, even motor highways. Most of the old paths were so well situated that there was little reason to forsake them until the age of the automobile. That the Indians, taking every advantage offered by the terrain, "kept the level" so well among Pennsylvania's mountains is an engineering complexity of the system and its adaptability to changing seasons and weather. Colonial travelers and Indians met frequently on the trail. Whether traveling to hunt, trade, war, negotiate or visit, Native Americans demonstrated in these chance encounters that they were not the fiend some thought them to be.

—Paul A. W. Wallace, Indian Paths of Pennsylvania[8]

Many today do not know the extent of Indian Paths across the Commonwealth of Pennsylvania or the importance of the Paths that eventually became bridle paths, wagon roads, and motor highways for white society.

According to Paul A.W. Wallace of the Pennsylvania Historic and Museum Commission,

> *Most Indian paths were so well planned that, until the invention of the internal combustion engine, there was little occasion for any but minor changes in the route. Today, the discomfort caused by driving over frost-*

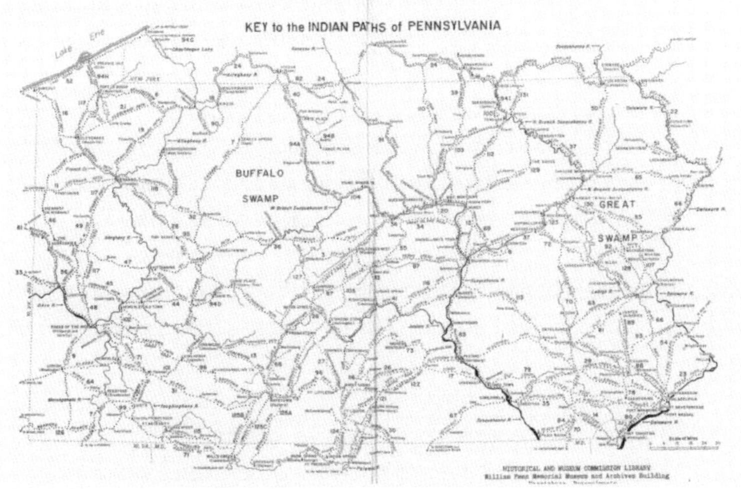

Key to publication, "Indian Paths of Pennsylvania," by Paul A.W. Wallace.
Courtesy of the Pennsylvania Historic and Museum Commission, Harrisburg, Pennsylvania.

> *broken roads, which had diverged from the Indian's dry ridge routes, is a reminder of how good a road engineer the Indian was.... Those words, dry, level, and direct, give the key to Indian path making. They were dry for the most part because they followed river terraces above flood level, or because they followed—especially in the soft coal country—well drained ridges.... In Western Pennsylvania, where much of the country is cut up into a jumble of hills and glens, the Indian paths followed the highest ridges because they alone offered a level course. Such were the Big Level in McKean and Elk counties.... It was not everywhere possible for the traveler to keep his moccasins dry. Rivers and Creeks had to be forded.*[9]

Early settlers followed the Indian paths into the Pennsylvania Wilds region. As an example, the trip in one section of the Great Shamokin Path, which passed from Clearfield to Punxsutawney, was not an easy one.

> *Between Chinklacamoose* [Clearfield] *and the mouth of Anderson Creek (Curwensville), several crossings of the Susquehanna were made necessary, as Harold Woolridge has noted, in order to escape the high laurel bushes, which were a nightmare to travel.*[10]

This path was also recorded by Bishop John Ettwein, who took this route with his two hundred Indians and their cows in 1772.

> *Ettwein and his party camped in a "narrow and stony spot" at the mouth of Anderson Creek (Curwensville). Next morning, they left the West Branch and traveled "three miles to the northwest up the creek, crossing it five times." Here, the path went precipitately up the mountain.*[11]

Eventually, the Great Shamokin Path continued west through present-day Chestnut Grove, on to Luthersburg (Route 219), both in Clearfield County. It then followed today's Route 410.

> *Past the Big Spring, making its way toward present-day Troutville, Jefferson County* [now Amish Country]. *By the time the road reaches Troutville, the modern road is ½ mile or more west of the path. About two miles beyond Troutville, road and path come together again. In another 1½ miles, 410 merges with U.S. 119 for the next dozen miles. At Bells Mills, U.S. 119 leaves the Shamokin Path (which ran through Cloe) and passes through Punxsutawney.*[12]

It should be noted that two hundred years ago, settlers who used the Indian paths would have viewed painted trees.

> *It was an Indian custom to strip a ring of bark from a tree and paint on the exposed surface, with red ochre and charcoal, the news of the day. These tree paintings remained visible, sometimes for as long as fifty years. All Indians of Pennsylvania, whatever their spoken language, could read these pictures, which usually told about the exploits of hunters or a war party, although they were also used for other purposes. During the Braddock campaign* [French and Indian War], *the French Indians painted trees (where the British were bound to see them) with "many threats and bravados."*[13]

Indian paths were busy places. Settlers in earlier days frequently met Indians on the trail.

> *Whether they were engaged in hunting, trade, war, diplomacy, visiting relatives across the mountains, or going as onlookers to some treaty, these encounters proved them not to be the fiends nineteenth-century novelists*

collected dimes for persuading the public they were.... When white men met a party of Indians, it was good form to sit down with them under a tree and smoke a friendly pipe, meanwhile, exchanging the news of the day. If the young men of the Indian party had been hunting, it was likely they would press upon the strangers a haunch of venison or a gammon of bear's meat. Hospitality was a prime virtue among these people, whether in their homes or on the trail.[14]

3.

Penn's Woods

To understand the settlement of the region designated as the Pennsylvania Wilds, one needs to understand the colonial history of the commonwealth, beginning with the acquisition of the lands named Pennsylvania by William Penn, his dealings with the Native Americans, the French and Indian War and, subsequently, the American Revolution. The recognition of this history explains the boldness of those who first settled the Pennsylvania Wilds.

The commonwealth was founded by William Penn in 1644. The name Pennsylvania roughly translates to "Penn's Woods," by combining the Penn surname (in honor of William's father, Admiral Sir William Penn) with the Latin word *sylvania*, meaning "forest land." The king of England owed a debt to Penn's father, and Penn accepted the land that became known as the Colony of Pennsylvania and as a haven for those who, like him, were followers of the Quaker faith, which became the dominate ethnic group in Pennsylvania. Other English people of Anglican faith also settled Pennsylvania, with a large English population centered in the southeastern counties of Pennsylvania. By 1755, frontier life had given way to cosmopolitan life, with Philadelphia becoming a great center for Colonial America.[15]

Newspaper accounts of the day reveal the extent of the good life that was being enjoyed in Philadelphia. One advertisement proclaimed:

> *Imported, and to be sold by James Eddy, at his house, opposite Black-Horse-Alley, in Second Street, Fine Frontenack wine by the bottle or dozen,*

> *best wine vinegar, rum by the quart or gallon, tea and sugar, rice, felt hats… pencils and tools…English crown glass 8 by 10, 9 by 11…samplers, clock faces…and a large assortment of fine tiles for chimneys, cheap for ready money.* (October 1755)[16]

Another advertisement:

> *John Ormsby, who lately arrived from Norfolk, in Virginia, begs leave to acquaint the publick* [sic] *that he intends to open a FENCING and DANCING SCHOOL, next Monday, at the Large Room in Second Street, formerly called Mr. Vidal's Room, and where the late Mr. Quin kept his dancing school. FENCING ON Mondays, Wednesdays and Fridays in the forenoon for two dollars a month at the time of entrance. DANCING on the aforesaid days to begin at three in the afternoon for the benefit of tender children, who may be dismissed in the evening or continue till the school is dismissed at nine, for a quarter, and the same at entrance.* (Philadelphia, October 16, 1755)[17]

Life on the Pennsylvania frontier was much different from the cosmopolitan life enjoyed by the residents of Philadelphia. The frontier was settled by Germans and Scotch-Irish colonists. The abundance of wildlife in the wilderness led many of these settlers to earn their living as packmen, hunting and selling animal pelts; while others became farmers. Wolves, panthers, bears and other wild animals prowled the forests where those colonists were living.

Frontier women bore the load along with their husbands and children. Supplies were located miles away from their homesteads. Women's days consisted of grinding meal; cooking; baking bread; salting meat for preservation; preserving other foods; attending to the vegetable gardens that were staples of frontier life; caring for children; and carrying out chores, such as feeding chickens and milking cows. The women also made clothes for the family members, and water for the families' use had to be hauled from nearby springs. Washing clothes was another matter—the woman of the house may have carried clothes to a nearby creek, or if she had a large tub, she would build a fire outdoors to heat water with which she washed and rinsed the clothes. Frontier women were also known to plow alongside their husbands and help fell trees for cabin building. Cabins were commonly made from round logs with clapboard roofs secured by beams.

With the arrival of waves of settlers, the Delaware Indians had been driven west into Pennsylvania from other colonies, where they became involved in the fur trade. In dealing with the white settlers, the Indians often reminded them that William Penn had pledged he would always treat the Indians peacefully and fairly.

William Penn, through his faith as a pacifist Quaker, did practice fair treatment of the Indians. Penn understood their claims to land ownership. And although the Indians may not have always recognized the purchase of lands as a white settler did, Penn, nevertheless, bought lands through negotiation—the very lands that had been granted to him by the crown. Through what was described by the two sides as the "chain of friendship," William Penn and the Indians had sixty years of peace, a longer-lasting peace than the fifty years of peace enjoyed by the Mayflower Pilgrims and their Native neighbors.

Laws were passed during William Penn's lifetime to prevent the Indians from being taken advantage of in land purchases. Permission to buy land from the Indians had to come from the proprietary. But with vast numbers of settlers arriving, the government eventually recognized squatters' rights.

William Penn died in 1718. Penn's sons, John, Richard and Thomas, inherited the colony's proprietorship but lived beyond their means. In order to satisfy their debts, they chose not to follow through on Penn's chain of friendship, but rather, they began selling land to European settlers before it had been purchased from the Indians, as had been their father's custom.

As more and more Europeans moved into Pennsylvania, officials believed they needed to get clear title to the lands they were settling. The officials showed the Delaware Indians a deed that asserted Penn had purchased certain lands in 1686. The Delaware Indians had moved into the region of Pennsylvania in question from New Jersey and didn't know anything about the deed. The land described in this so-called deed had never been measured to the satisfaction of buyer or seller. In other words, the claim by the Penn family was questionable.

This negotiation eventually led to one of the largest land grabs in the history of Pennsylvania, the Walking Purchase. In 1737, to measure the purchase and establish boundaries, it was said that the deed indicated that the purchase "extended from a point on the Delaware River near present-day Wrightstown, northwest into the interior 'as far as a Man could walk in a day and a half' a typical Indian measurement of space."[18]

The Walking Purchase was a fraud. The phrase "as far as a Man could walk in a day and a half" was measured for the government by three hired walkers. Two of the three dropped out. The third collapsed in exhaustion. The Delaware walkers withdrew early, complaining that the white men were

Oil painting, *The Treaty of Penn with the Indians*, completed 1771–72 by Benjamin West. *Courtesy of the State Museum of Pennsylvania.*

not fair. In the end, surveyors drew a line to the Upper Delaware River, near the New York border, granting much more land to the government than what the Delaware had understood would be conveyed. A piece of land roughly the size of the state of Rhode Island, 1,200,932 acres, was transferred to the Pennsylvania government.

When William Penn came to Pennsylvania, the Delaware occupied southeastern Pennsylvania, but their political overlords were the Iroquois through the Iroquois Confederacy, which originally consisted of five tribes but eventually came to include the Delaware Nation. Following the Walking Purchase, with the Delaware refusing to leave the land, the proprietary government sought the intervention of the Iroquois Confederacy. The Delaware, appealing to the confederacy over the sale of the land, were not supported by them. The Iroquois, apparently believing it was not in their best interest politically to intervene, stated the Delaware had no right to sell the land in the first place. The Delaware people, recognizing the Iroquois Confederacy's authority over them, were forced off the land in 1741.

By 1741, in other areas of Pennsylvania where the Indians did have ownership, they complained about white settlers trespassing on that land.[19] Eventually, to satisfy Indian complaints, the government ordered the settlers

Left: Oil painting, *Lapowinsa, a Delaware Chief, 1735*, by Gustauvus Hesselius. Lapowinsa was a Delaware chief involved in selling land through the controversial Walking Purchase Agreement. *Courtesy of the Library of Congress, National Portrait Gallery, Smithsonian Institution.*

Right: Oil painting, *Tishcohan, a Delaware Chief, 1735*, by Gustauvus Hesselius. Tishcohan a Delaware chief involved in selling land through the controversial Walking Purchase agreement. *Courtesy of the Library of Congress, National Portrait Gallery, Smithsonian Institution.*

off the land. The result of that order was the burning of cabins at a settlement known as Sydneyville. Subsequently rebuilt, the new village bore the name reflecting its recent history, Burnt Cabins.

An account of the confrontation described the event.

> *On May 24, 1750, Conrad Weiser found himself facing the loaded gun of Andrew Lycon, a Scots-Irish squatter on Indian-owned land in the Juniata Valley. Weiser, who had agreed to accompany colonial secretary Richard Peters and some local magistrates into this frontier region as their Indian interpreter, must have wondered what he had gotten himself into. Like the colonial officials he was working for, Weiser considered squatters such as Lycon backcountry riff-raff, troublemakers who stirred up hostilities with Indians and refused to cooperate with colonial authorities. If peace was going to be preserved on the Pennsylvania frontier, Lycon and his neighbors had to go.*[20]

Lycon had his own ideas about the land, possibly fueled by the Irish resistance to Britain in their own homeland. "From his perspective, Weiser and his party were tools of the Penn family, wealthy proprietors who lived in England and took no interest in the hard work or livelihoods of frontier families who made Pennsylvania a prosperous colony."[21]

It appears that the Penn family hoped to profit from the eventual sale of these lands. The settlers…objected to their treatment because the Penn family had encouraged them to settle there years earlier to assert Pennsylvania possession of territory claimed by Maryland.…Burning of the cabins did little to forestall the tide of Scots-Irish emigrants crossing the Susquehanna." The settlers soon returned to the land where their homes had been burned. "Just five months after their expedition across the Tuscarora Mountains… the People over the Hills are comdin'd against the Government, [and] are putting new crops and bid us defiance."[22]

Pressures mounted between the proprietary government and the Indians. By October 16, 1755, the British Colonies were gripped in conflict with the French and Natives, and the first of many Indian attacks against the colonials in Pennsylvania took place in what is known as the Penn's Creek Massacre.

Part II

THE FRENCH AND INDIAN WAR

4.

A Young George Washington

The conflict was the last of a series of wars between Great Britain and France for control of North America. Known in Europe as the Seven Years' War, the conflict began when Britain and France declared war on each other in 1756 and ended when they made peace in 1763. But in America, the war raged in colonial Pennsylvania between 1754 and 1764 (which included Pontiac's Rebellion in 1763) and has also been known as the Old French War, or, the more recognized name to most in American history, the French and Indian War.

Much of the friction had been over possession of Canada, New England, the New York frontier and the Caribbean Islands. By the mid-eighteenth century, the French were moving into the Ohio Valley in an effort to link Canada with their possessions in Louisiana and the Mississippi Valley.

In 1753, the lieutenant governor of Virginia Robert Dinwiddie was calling on the British government to stop the French from entering the Ohio Valley. George Washington, hearing about these efforts and possibly hoping to make a name for himself by coming to the attention of Dinwiddie, traveled to Williamsburg, Virginia, to volunteer to be Britain's emissary to the French. Dinwiddie received Washington, listened to his proposal to become Britain's emissary to the French and accepted the young and somewhat inexperienced George Washington. Washington was to set out with a small expedition to warn the French to stop trespassing on British claims in the Ohio Valley. He journeyed from Virginia to Wills Creek, Cumberland, Maryland, where he hired Christopher Gist as a guide. From

Oil painting, *Colonel George Washington, 1772*, by Charles Wilson Peale, donated to Washington and Lee University in 1897. *Courtesy of Wikimedia Commons.*

there, he hired porters to take them to Logstown, a Native settlement north of today's city of Pittsburgh.

At Logstown, Washington met with an Indian man known as "Half King," whose name was Tanacharison. Presenting gifts, Washington hoped to convince Tanacharison to join him. Having his own grievances against the French, he agreed to accompany Washington. Eventually reaching the Allegheny River, the expedition went north to Fort Venango. The French commander there refused to accept the letter that Washington was carrying from Dinwiddie. Instead, Washington was sent up Venango, or French Creek, to Fort Le Beouf, where he held a conference with the French commandant St. Pierre.

Indian trails played a major role in Washington's journey, and it is very likely that Washington and company made their trek from Logstown to Fort LeBeouf over the Logstown and Venango Paths and north to Fort LeBoeuf.

The message that Washington carried from Dinwiddie, the governor of Virginia, was widely reported in the newspapers of the day:

> *Copy of Governor DINWIDDIE's Letter to the Commandant of the French Forces on the Ohio, sent by Major Washington.*
>
> *SIR,*
>
> *The lands upon the River Ohio, in the western parts of the colony of Virginia, are so notoriously known to be the property of the Crown of Great-Britain, that it is a matter of equal concern and surprize* [sic] *to me, to hear that a body of French Forces are erecting fortresses, and making settlements upon that river, within His Majesty's dominions.*
>
> *The many and repeated complaints I have receiv'd of these acts of hostility, lay me under the necessity of sending, in the name of the king my master, the bearer hereof, George Washington, Esq; one of the adjutants general of the forces of this dominion, to complain to you of the encroachments thus made, and of the injuries done to the subjects of Great-Britain, in open violation of the Law of Nations, and the treaties now subsisting between the two Crowns.*
>
> *If these facts are true, and you shall think fit to justify your proceedings, I must desire you to acquaint me, by whose authority and instructions you have lately marched from Canada, with an arm'd force, and invaded the King of Great-Britain's Territories, and the manner complain'd of; that according to the purport and resolution of your answer, I may act agreeably to the commission I am honour'd with from the king my master.*
>
> *However, sir, in obedience to my instructions, it becomes my duty to require your peaceable departure; and that you would forbear prosecuting a purpose so interruptive of the harmony and good understanding, which His Majesty is desirous to continue and cultivate with the most Christian king.*

I persuade myself, you will receive and entertain Major Washington with the candour and politeness natural to your nation; and it will give me the greatest satisfaction, if you return him with an answer suitable to my wishes for a very long, and lasting peace between us. I have the honour to subscribe myself,

Sir,
Your most obedient humble Serrvant [sic],
Robert Dinwiddie
October 31, 1753, Williamsburg, in Virginia[23]

The answer from the French Commandant was translated into English:

SIR,

As I have the honour to command here in chief, Mr. Washington delivered me the letter which you directed to the commandant of the French troops. I should have been pleased if you had given him orders, or if he himself had been disposed to visit Canada, and our general, to whom, rather than to me, it properly appertains, to demonstrate the reality of the king of my master's rights to the lands situated along the Ohio, and to dispute the pretentions of the king of Great-Britain in that respect.

I shall immediately forward your letter to Monsieur Le Marquis Duquisne; his answer will be a law to me: and if he directs me to communicate it to you, I assure you, sir, I shall neglect nothing that may be necessary to convey it to you with expedition.

As to the requisition you make, that I retire (with the troops under my command) I cannot believe myself under any obligation to submit to it. I am here in virtue of my general's orders; and I beg, sir, you would not doubt a moment of my fix'd resolution to conform to them, with all the exactitude and steadiness that might be expected from a better officer.

I do not know that, in the course of this campaign, any thing [sic] *has passed that can be esteemed an act of hostility, or contrary to the treaties subsisting between the two crowns, the continuation of which is as interesting and pleasing to us as it can be to the English. If it had been agreeable to you, sir, in this respect, to have made a particular detail of the facts which occasion your complaint, I should have had the honour of answering you in the most explicit manner, and I am persuaded you would have had reason to be satisfied.*

I have taken particular care to receive Mr. Washington with all the distinction suitable to your dignity, and to his quality and great merit. I flatter myself that he will do me this justice and join me in testifying the profound respect with which I am,

Sir,
From the Fort at Beef River, Your most humble, and most obedient Servant,
Legardeur De St. Pierre
December 15, 1753[24]

Rejecting the British demands, the French, in 1754, moved to take control of a half-built British fort at the forks of the Ohio River in what is today the city of Pittsburgh. The site was named Fort Duquesne by the French. To counteract their claim, another expedition, again headed by George Washington, was sent to the Ohio Valley, where he built a stockade known as Fort Necessity. From this location, Washington and his militia challenged the French but were defeated and forced to surrender on July 3, 1754. That battle was the beginning of the French and Indian War for colonial Pennsylvania.

5.

General Braddock

General Braddock joined the military at an early age, following in his father's footsteps. Born in Perthshire, Scotland, in January 1695, he made his way through the ranks when, in 1754, he was made major-general. Appointed to command against the French in America, Braddock landed with two regiments of British regulars in February 1755 in Hampton, Virginia.

In April 1755, General Braddock met with several colonial governors who urged him to take action against the French. He began to make preparations to take Fort Duquesne from the French and to win back control of the Ohio Valley.

The French had a long history with the Indians, and they relied on the Indians as a basis for their economy, particularly in the fur trade. The British were interested in settlements and wanted to secure more land to be sold to the settlers. The Delaware Indians could have backed either side. Even after their difficulties with claims to their land, the Indians leaned toward siding with the British against the French. In the end, they sided with the French. Their decision may have been very different without General Braddock's attitude toward the Indians. Shingas, a Delaware chief, met with Braddock before Braddock's campaign to capture Fort Duquesne. Shingas sought a guarantee from Braddock: should the Indians who followed Shingas support Braddock against the French, he asked that Braddock vacate the Ohio Valley so they could retain the land for themselves. Braddock, possibly not understanding the importance of having this Indian backing, told Shingas

A mortally wounded Edward Braddock being carried from battlefield on July 9, 1755. *Woodcarving from 1836, courtesy of the Library of Congress.*

that he was going to secure the Ohio for the British king and stay there as long as the king wanted him to, further stating, "No savage should inherit the land."[25] He also said he would drive the French and their Indians away without the help of Shingas and his warriors. Braddock's arrogance cost him his life and the lives of many settlers on the Pennsylvania frontier.

On July 9, 1755, Braddock and his militia, with just a few Indian allies, marched on Fort Duquesne in an attempt to regain possession of the fort. They were defeated by the French. Braddock was wounded and died on July 13. George Washington had accompanied him on this expedition. Braddock's failure left the frontiers of Pennsylvania, Maryland and Virginia open to attack by the French and their Indian allies.

On July 24, 1755, the General Assembly of the Province of Pennsylvania met at Philadelphia, where a speech describing the situation of Braddock's defeat was given by Robert Hunter Morris, the lieutenant governor of the province of Pennsylvania and the counties of New Castle, Kent and Suffix upon the Delaware:

> *Mr. Speaker, and Gentlemen of the Assembly, it is with the greatest concern I now lay before you the melancholy accounts of the defeat of the forces under the immediate command of General Braddock, which you will find is attended with very shocking circumstances; the general killed, and most of the officers that were in the action, are either killed or wounded, the bulk of the men cut off, his whole train of artillery taken, and Colonel Dunbar is now retreating with the remains of the army to Fort Cumberland. This unfortunate and unexpected change in our affairs will deeply affect every one of His Majesty's Colonies, but none of them in so sensible a manner as this province, which having no militia, is thereby left exposed to the cruel incursions of the French, and their barbarous Indians, who delight in shedding human blood, and who make no distinction as to age or sex—as to those that are armed against them, or such as they can surprise in their peaceful habitations—all are alike the objects of their cruelty—slaughtering the tender infant and frightened mother with equal joy and fierceness. To such enemies, spurred on by the native cruelty of their tempers, encouraged by their late successes, and having now no army to fear, are the inhabitants of this province exposed; and by such must we now expect to be over-run, if we do not immediately prepare for our own defence* [sic]. *Nor ought we to content ourselves with this, but resolve to drive and confine the French to their just limits.*
>
> *This, gentlemen, however gloomy the present appearance of things may be, is certainly in the power of the British Colonies to do, and this is not only their truest and most lasting interest but their highest duty.*[26]

The smug attitude of British officers, as demonstrated by General Braddock, continued throughout the war.

6.

General Jeffrey Amherst

By 1757, the tide began to turn for the British after they sent a number of young aggressive British generals to North America. One of those officers was General Jeffrey Amherst, who was commanding general of the British forces in North America. He is credited with the success of conquering the French during the French and Indian War.

Amherst was born in Sevenoaks, England, in 1717. His family included distinguished military men. His brothers were Admiral John Amherst and Lieutenant General William Amherst. Amherst saw action in several locations in his early career, including Germany in 1756. In 1761, he was appointed Knight of the Order of Bath.

Under his command in 1759, the British were having more success against the French, defeating them on the Plains of Abraham above Quebec. In 1761, the British captured Montreal. Challenged by the French, the British remained in control of all of Canada. In the Caribbean, the British took most of the French sugar islands. The war in the Caribbean continued through 1762, with the Spanish joining the French to fight the British.

A peace treaty known as the Treaty of Paris of 1763 was signed on February 10, 1763, by Great Britain, France and Spain, giving the British control of Canada, Acadia, the eastern half of the Mississippi Valley and Florida, which was exchanged by the Spanish for Cuba, as Great Britain had taken it in 1762.

At the end of the war, France was no longer a colonial power in North America. It retained two small islands in the Gulf of St. Lawrence and

Jeffrey Amherst, the first Baron Amherst, circa 1765. *Print of painting by Joshua Reynolds, courtesy of the Library of Congress.*

fishing rights off Newfoundland. Earlier, France had ceded New Orleans and the western portion of its Mississippi Valley Territory to Spain.

In an earlier chapter, it was noted that Conrad Weiser, in his dealings with the Scotch-Irish settlers, considered them backcountry riffraff and troublemakers.

This was also the view of the British officers, including Amherst, who were disparaging of the Indians as well. In correspondence to Sir William Johnson during Pontiac's Rebellion (1763–1764), Amherst wrote:

> *It would be happy for the provinces there was not an Indian settlement within a thousand miles of them, and when they are properly punished, I care not how soon they move their habitations, for the inhabitants of the woods are the fittest companions for them, they being more nearly allied to the brute than to the human creation.*[27]

Amherst's callous attitude against the Indians is discussed in a later chapter concerning the use of germ warfare against them during Pontiac's Rebellion. With all of Amherst's achievements, he is remembered, at least in this country, for advocating for the use of germ warfare.

7.

Shingas

A Delaware Sachem

The Lenni Lenape tribe, known to white settlers as the Delaware, was the tribe most closely associated with Pennsylvania, its name meaning the real (or original) people.[28]

Pennsylvania's Indians at the time white settlers were arriving in the area were in the woodland phase of development. Research reveals they were living in towns, making good pottery and were artistic in their decoration of their leather garments and blankets. Singing and dancing also accompanied their religious rituals.[29]

Delaware Indians were not bound by a government as modern Americans understand social order. Their organization followed their maternal lineage, which consisted of a group of people descended from common ancestors exclusively through the female line. Each lineage had its own chief or sachem.[30]

> *Three types of kinship have been described: (1) The single (nuclear) family: mother, father, and their children; (2) The lineage: a woman with her descendants in the female line; (3) The clan: a group of lineages all tracing descent from a remote or mythical ancestor, often an animal or bird, whose name the clan bore. The Delaware had three clans—Turtle, Turkey, and Wolf—representatives of which could be found in any community.*[31]

The Delaware religion believed in the Great Spirit, the creator. Described by a Delaware Indian who claimed to have seen him as a great man, "He was clothed with the day; yea, with the brightest day he ever saw…this whole world...was drawn upon him, so that in him, the earth, and all things on it, might be seen."[32]

The Indians' religion shaped their view on land ownership. "Their belief was that both the land and animals that roamed the forest had been given by the Creator for the common use and were not to be regarded as anyone's private property."[33] "'What', said Tecumseh, 'Sell land! As well sell air and water. The Great Spirit gave them in common to all.'"[34]

To understand Tecumseh's thought process might be to understand the story of the creation and the role the turtle played in it. In a description of a woman who fell to earth through an opening in heaven, according to the story, as she approached a great expanse of water, birds gathered and held her up out of the water. Looking around, they chose a mud turtle to keep her safe and deposited her on his back. Animals dived into the water to find a bit of soil for the turtle's back. As time went on, the soil and the turtle began to grow. "Soon there was enough land for the woman to walk about on. The mud turtle then said to the woman, 'I will remain forever to support you and all the generations that are to come. These commands I have received from above.'"[35] The turtle clan were the keepers of the earth.

It was these two diverging points of view—the colonials' need for expansion into new lands to raise crops to live on the land and the Natives' spiritual connection to the land, which they believed was common to all—that became the backdrop of the French and Indian War in Pennsylvania.

The World on the Turtle's Back, by John Fadden. *From* Indians in Pennsylvania, *by Paul A.W. Wallace, published by the Pennsylvania Historic and Museum Commission.*

Shingas, was a member of the Turkey Clan, and as such, he was a leading chief (sachem) of the Turkey Clan. In mythology, the turkey is said to be "stationary and always remains with or about them."[36] But circumstances caused Shingas to be on the move.

The position of chief over the Delaware Nation, through long-standing tradition, was only open to members of the Turtle Clan. The Pennsylvania government used the title "king" to refer to the chief. After the death of Delaware chief Sassoonan, who was Shingas's uncle, the position of head chief was vacant. The Pennsylvania government had been able to manipulate

Sassoonan over the years, leading him to sign away Native lands, and was looking for another chief they could easily influence. Shingas's brother Pisquetomen was designated Sassoonan's successor, but because he was strong and not subject to colonial influence, the Pennsylvania officials refused to recognize him. As a result, Pisquetomen, along with Shingas and their brother Tamaqua, abandoned Pennsylvania, leading their people over the Allegheny Mountains, that physical barrier, to settle at Kittanning on the Allegheny River.[37]

With no recognized chief for five years, in 1752, Tanacharison, the Iroquois half king (the Iroquois had authority over the Delaware), appointed Shingas as chief. He remained head chief until 1758, when he was placed on the British government's most wanted list and replaced by his brother Tamaqua.[38]

While no written physical appearance of Shingas has been found, William Penn himself provided a description of the Delaware Indians in a letter to the Free Society of Traders in 1685.

> *For their persons, they are generally tall, straight, well-built, and of singular proportion; they tread strong and clever, and mostly walk with a lofty chin: of complexion, black, but by design, as the Gypsies in England: they grease themselves with bears-fat clarified, and using no defence* [sic] *against sun or weather, their skins must needs be swarthy; their eye is little and black, not unlike a straight-look't Jew: the thick lip and flat nose, so frequent with the East-Indians and Blacks, are not common to them; for I have seen a comely European-like faces among them of both, as on your side of the sea; and truly an Italian complexion hath not much more of the white, and the noses of several of them have as much of the Roman.*[39]

In summer, Shingas and his warriors dressed simply, wearing a belt, breechcloth and moccasins. As the seasons changed, so did their dress. In winter, they wore robes of skins from deer, bears, beavers and raccoons, with deerskin jackets draped over their shoulders. They wore leggings fastened with thongs to waist-belts from above their knees to below their ankles. Their clothing was decorated with designs of shell beads and porcupine quills. In their physical appearance, the Indians were partial to bright-red paint for their faces and bear's grease for the hair.[40] Long feathers were worn in their hair, but only by the men. The number of feathers and the angle at which they were worn were said to have indicated the tribe a man belonged to, and with the Delaware, usually only one or two feathers were worn.[41] Although

Oil on canvas, *Shingas, Sakima and Ila, (Chief and Warrior), Lenape Turkey Clan, circa 1740. By Ruth Major, with advice of Jim Rementer, the secretary of the Culture Preservation Committee, Delaware Tribe.*

some Indians had beards, their face hair was thin, and they would have pulled out what little they may have had. It was also their practice to pull out the hair on their heads so only a little remained on the crown of the head. This was known as the scalp lock. A symbol of manhood, it was carefully tended to during times of war.[42]

Shingas had a wife who died in 1762. In the world of the Delaware Natives, women had highly respected positions in the community, more than European women enjoyed at that time.

> *She owned the house, its equipment and the fields attached to it. In case of divorce, she kept the children. In public affairs, her advice was powerful.... She nursed the children, made the pottery, tanned the hides, dressed the game her husband brought, kept the fire burning, made the bread, provided her husband and family with two good meals a day, and kept a kettle of soup on the fire for possible visitors. She gathered the firewood, fetched the water, and made clothing for herself and the family. She plowed the ground, planted the corn, cultivated it, gathered it, and ground it into flour or meal.*[43]

While the day-to-day tasks of the Native women seemed to match the tasks undertaken by the women on the Pennsylvania frontier during those early years, the fact that Native women had "ownership" of their homes, equipment and fields differed greatly from their European counterparts, who had no inheritance rights under English law.

8.

Penn's Creek Massacre

Relations with the Indians continued to deteriorate as they lost more of their lands to colonists. Driven by their alliance with the French and fueled by Braddock's defeat, the first in a series of attacks by the Indians on the frontier settlements began at a place along the Susquehanna River known as Penn's Creek. A narrative from two girls who were taken captive in that attack, Marie LeRoy and Barbara Leininger, was written after their release from captivity.

Marie LeRoy, born in Brondrut, Switzerland, came with her family to Pennsylvania, settling in Union County around 1750. "Her father, John Jacob LeRoy, was a dyer of wool, and before his immigration to America was a resident of the beautiful Pays de Vaud in Switzerland…being on the border of France and Switzerland."[44] A half mile away from the LeRoy plantation, Barbara Leininger lived with her parents, who came from Reutlingen, Germany, to Pennsylvania around 1745.[45]

Early in the morning of October 16, 1755, as Leroy's hired man went out to bring in the cows, he heard six shots. Soon after, eight Indians came to the house, killed Marie LeRoy's father with a tomahawk, and while her brother defended himself, he was soon overpowered and taken prisoner along with Marie and a little girl who was staying with the family. The Indians then plundered the homestead and set it on fire.[46]

At the Leininger home, two Indians arrived, surprising Mr. Leininger; his two daughters, Barbara and Regina; and his son. The Indians demanded

Penn's Creek Massacre Historic Marker, circa June 5, 2011. *Courtesy of Paul Crumlish and www.hmdb.org.*

rum and tobacco. In the narrative of the attack, the Indians' message was: "We are Allegheny Indians, and you are our enemies. You must all die."[47] Barbara's brother and father were killed, and Barbara and her sister, Regina, were taken captive and joined the other Indians, who had Marie LeRoy and the little boy in custody. There were fourteen horses and ten prisoners (one man, one woman, five girls and three boys).

Back in Philadelphia an ominous warning appeared in the newspaper, recounting the massacre:

> *Extract of a letter from Lancaster County, dated Oct. 28, 1755:*
>
> *As I imagine you have been alarmed before this time, with a great deal of bad news from these parts, I think it my duty to give you as much light into the affair as I can—About the 20th instant, news was brought that the French and Indians had actually massacred and scalped a number of our inhabitants, not more than 40 miles from Harris's Ferry—It is reasonable to think the receipt of such news must put the inhabitants in the utmost confusion. About 45 of the stoutest of them got themselves mounted and in readiness the next day to go and bury the dead; they reached the place, accordingly, and found no less than 14 bodies most shockingly mangled—while they were in this place, some friendly Indians, who were flying to the inhabitants for protection, told them there were a large body of French and Indians actually on their march to the inhabited parts of this province, and were already on this side of the Allegheny Mountains; upon this, they concluded to go as far as Shamokin, to know whether the Indians assembled there were friends or enemies (for our people supposed these Indians to have some knowledge of the murder) and to get, if possible, further intelligence about those they had heard were advancing toward them.*[48]

The article concludes with the information that the Delaware Indians were responsible for the attack and that the court house bell had been ringing continuously to notify the inhabitants to seek safety.

9.

Great Cove Massacre

A second attack, the attack on the Great Cove, was led by the Delaware chief, Shingas. With a party of about one hundred Shawnees and Delaware Indians, they entered Great Cove, massacring most of its inhabitants while carrying others off into captivity.

It was the custom of warring Indians to apply face paint—black signaling evil, grief and death. We can surmise that Shingas, along with his Delaware accomplice, Tewa (Captain Jacob), were thus painted as they drew near the area of the Great Cove: black faces over their favorite vermillion (red) base, their eyes circled with black to enhance an evil appearance. Those who accompanied Shingas and Captain Jacob on this raiding party were most likely volunteers who were recruited at war dances.[49] Their intent was clearly to strike fear into the hearts of the settlers they attacked, hoping to move them off the land.

To inflict terror in the population under attack, the Indians would let out "the sharp, high-pitched war whoop (variously called also the death halloo, death whoop, death cry, and scalp cry)" prior to and during the attack.[50]

So, on November 1, 1755, just days after a newspaper article appeared in the *Pennsylvania Gazette* warning of the Indian attack at Penn's Creek, William Fleming was about seven miles from home when a man named Burns repeated a rumor of an imminent Indian attack. While some thought the rumor was foolish due to good relations between the settlers and Indians in that Province, Fleming decided to not be foolhardy. Turning his horse in the direction of his home, he rode quickly, planning to take his pregnant wife to the nearest fort for safety.[51] Within two miles of his home, two Indians jumped out from behind some trees and took hold of his horse's bridle. In good English, they ordered Fleming off the horse, shook his hand and forced him to go with them. As he recounted in his later narrative, Fleming was speechless and trembling. His captors, apparently sensing his fear, assured him they would not hurt him if he would go with them. One of the Indians was the aforementioned Captain Jacob (Tewa), the leader of the attack with Shingas.[52]

On his way to his home with the Indians, Fleming passed a homestead that was owned by the Hicks family. Hoping that the family would be alerted and offer him a chance for escape, he saw two of the Hicks's sons leave their home after dinner. As they walked out of the house, the Indians quickly went after them. One son ran back into the house, while the other youth was taken to join Fleming in captivity. He screamed for help, but no one came out of the house.[53]

William Fleming had the good sense to keep his wits about him as he traveled toward his home with the Indians and the Hicks captive. Captain Jacob told Fleming that the Indians had need of a cook and that, while it had been determined before the attack to take only young men and women as captives, Fleming's wife would be safe if she would act as cook.

The Hicks youth resisted, slowing their advance toward the Fleming house. Fleming recounted that the Indians tied him to a tree, and he witnessed the death of the young man at the hands of an Indian known as Jim. Jim seized the Hicks boy and gave him a blow on the back of his head with his tomahawk. Falling to the ground, Jim stood over him, waiting to see if there was any life left in him. When he saw movement in the boy, he took his hand, wiped the blood off of his face, which was blinding the young captive, took the tomahawk and struck a final fatal blow to his head.[54]

Leaving the Hicks youth lying on the ground, they moved quickly, soon arriving at the Fleming house. William, doing his best to keep his wife, Elizabeth, calm, reassured her of the Indians' pledge not to harm them if they cooperated with them. The Indians sacked the house and set it on fire. Returning to the Hicks's house, which, by this time, was empty, the Indians ransacked it and set it on fire.

While following their captors, Elizabeth Fleming, at one point, summoned up the courage to ask them why they were attacking the settlers when they had always enjoyed good relations. The following is the narrative recounted by William Fleming:

> *My wife, being emboldened by the familiarity of our masters,* [Captain Jacob (Tewa) and Jim] *asked them several questions touching on their reasons for using the English as they did, seeing they had always treated the Indians (particularly the Delawares and Shawnees) with the greatest friendship. To which they answered, "When a number of Indians offered to join G—— B——* [General Braddock] *against the French, he did not use them well and had threatened to destroy all the Indians on the continent after they had conquered the French, and they* [the Indians] *were informed by the French* [that] *the Pennsylvanians, Marylanders and Virginians had laid the same plot."*[55]

Interestingly, the account recorded in the Fleming narrative is very similar to a speech attributed to Shingas, the Delaware chief who led the attack on the Coves, which was recorded by an Indian captive by the name of Charles Stuart, who was captured in a 1755 raid:

> *We, the Delawares of Ohio, do declare war against the English. We have been their friends many years but now have taken up the hatchet against them, and we will never make it up with them whilst there is an Englishman alive.*[56]

The Flemings were with their captors for less than a day before they made their escape. When the Indians fell into a deep sleep, William and Elizabeth made off into the woods; however, during their escape, they were separated. Without his wife, William Fleming made for Fort Conococheague, where he received reports that the Hicks family was attacked while fleeing to the nearest fortified house. Elizabeth soon joined her husband at the fort and recounted how, during her escape, she came across the dead body of her neighbor, John Hicks.[57]

What paths were used to take the prisoners of the Great Cove Massacre westward into Indian- and French-held territory? The Raystown Path, which ran west from Burnt Cabins (located approximately twelve miles north of the Great Cove) to the forks of the Ohio and Allegheny Rivers at present-day Pittsburgh, seems to have been one likely route. Another possibility is that the captives were taken northwest to the Kittanning Path, which eventually intersected with the Great Shamokin Path, making its way west, across Pennsylvania. Kittanning, in western Pennsylvania, otherwise known as Shingas Town, served as a center for processing captives. From there, prisoners were allocated to the various raiding groups. The raiders might have ceremonially tortured and killed some of the captives, while others might have been painted black to await execution on their return to the Ohio Valley.[58]

The remains of those who were killed at the Great Cove Massacre were buried at Big Spring Graveyard, near McConnellsburg in Fulton County, Pennsylvania. The following is the inscription on that location's historical marker:

> *Big Spring Graveyard*
> *Among those buried here are victims of the Great Cove Massacre of Nov. 1, 1755, at present McConnellsburg. The raid was conducted by Delawares and Shawnees led by Shingas, the Delaware "king." Houses were burned, and about 50 settlers were killed or captured. Its revelation at a meeting of Pennsylvania's Provincial Council, Nov. 5, 1755, led by Gov. R.H. Morris to ask the assembly for increased frontier protection.*

The attack was not successful in driving the settlers off the land and eventually led to the construction of a series of forts across the Pennsylvania frontier.

10.
Indian Captives

We learn from various accounts how the captive settlers were treated by the Indians. The main objective of bringing captives back to the Indian villages was to replace their deceased relatives. During the 1750s, Indians in the Ohio Valley had been wracked by several devastating smallpox epidemics. The acquisition of captives provided an easy means of maintaining tribal populations.[59]

In Paul A.W. Wallace's book *Indians in Pennsylvania*, he gave a fair description of the views on both sides of the story, the colonials and the Natives.

> *Stories of Indian captivities and tortures supplied the most popular reading, next to the Bible, of most Americans during the adolescent years of this nation and so helped to draw the people of thirteen separate colonies together in recognition of a common danger.*
>
> *Different peoples have different fashions in cruelty as well as in dress. It horrified white men to know that Indians, in the excitement of war, tortured some of their prisoners. It horrified Indians to know that white men ill-treated Indian women and sold their children into slavery. Today, as we look back upon Indian tortures, all of us—Indians and white men alike—are ashamed that humanity should have sunk so low. We are no less ashamed when we read of the tortures that were part of the normal judicial process in "civilized" countries as late as the seventeenth century—tortures used to extort the "confessions" that sent many innocent persons to the stake.*[60]

In a 2011 master's thesis titled "Determining Reliability in Indian Captivity Narratives," Heather Nicole DiAngelis from the College of William and Mary pointed out that many of the existing narratives were not written close to the time following the captivity. The narratives, for the most part, were from a male point of view, with few being provided from female captives. In those narratives to which credibility has been assigned, the captives shared similar stories: (1) adoption and degrees of assimilation; (2) running the gauntlet; (3) washing out the white; and (4) replacing family members.

DiAngelis made a study of eighteen narratives that involved twenty captives and determined the following:

> *The narratives concern Richard and Catharine Poe Bard, Thomas Brown, Robert Eastburn, William and Elizabeth Fleming, Thomas Gist, Henry Grace, Alexander Henry, William Henry, Isaac Hollister, Mary Jemison, James Johnson, Titus King, Jean Lowry, John McCullough, Charles Saunders, James Smith, Charles Stuart, and Peter Williamson. Each is unique, though all have common themes. Some describe aspects of Indian culture, some focus on warfare; others concentrate on "savage cruelty" while others describe the constant desire to return to white society. Some captives wrote about their experiences to inform the public about Indian ways of life, while others wrote merely for money; others did not write their own narrative. Some authors published their narratives immediately and solely for profit, while others waited decades to publish because their narratives were considered too tame for public interest.*[61]

Some captives eventually escaped, some were traded to the French as servants and others were returned to white society at the end of hostilities in negotiated settlements between the British and the Indians. What is known is that not all those who were redeemed wanted to go back to the white world, and some who were returned left, going back to the Indians and the lives they had grown comfortable with. Those who had been captured as children between the ages of three and six generally had no memory of their white lives and considered the adoptive Indians as their families. Older children, who had been captured between the ages of seven and fifteen, had memories of their former lives but were young enough to be made into "White Indians."[62]

11.

Mary Jemison

The story of captive Mary Jemison was written from interviews by James E. Sever when Mary was approximately eighty years old, sixty-eight years after she was taken into captivity. As she was only about twelve years old when she was captured, Mary was not clear about all of the details of her former life. Recounting that she and her family immigrated to Pennsylvania from Ireland, Mary was not sure if her parents lived in Scotland or Ireland, but she recalled their immigration was around 1742–43. Sever commented that when interviewing Mary, she retained her Irish brogue.

In the spring of 1755, Mary and her family, who were living in Adams County at the time, were attacked before breakfast by Indians. The first inkling the family had of the impending attack was the sound of gunshots. When they opened the door, they could see that the bodies of their neighbor and his horse were lying on the ground. The Indians had secured her father and pushed their way into the house, quickly taking the occupants inside captive. After plundering the house, Mary; her father; her mother; her brothers, Robert and Matthew; her sister, Betsy; and a woman and three children who were staying with them were hurried away into the woods. Two other brothers who had been hiding in the barn escaped.

The raiding party consisted of six Shawnee Indians and four Frenchmen. Mary described an Indian going behind them with a whip, frequently using it on the children to make them keep pace. The first night, there was no water or food for them, and they slept on the ground, unprotected from the elements.

Mary Jemison Historic Marker, Franklin Township, Adams County, Pennsylvania. *Courtesy of Wikimedia Commons.*

The next day, the captives were given a breakfast made from the provisions that had been taken from her parents' home. Moving on, the group stopped, sometime toward evening, near a swamp. There, one of the Indians took off Mary's stockings and shoes and put moccasins on her feet. They did the same with one young boy who was the son of the woman who had been staying in the Jemisons' home. Mary's mother, seeing what was happening, was said to have spoken these words to her daughter:

> *My dear little Mary, I fear that the time has arrived when we must be parted forever. Your life, my child, I think will be spared; but we shall probably be tomahawked here in this lonesome place by the Indians. O!*

> *How can I part with you, my darling? What will become of my sweet little Mary? Oh! How can I think of your being continued in captivity without a hope of your being rescued? O that death had snatched you from embraces in your infancy; the pain of parting then would have been pleasing to what it now is; and I should have seen the end of your troubles! Alas, my dear! My heart bleeds at the thoughts of what waits you; but, if you leave us, remember, my child, your own name, and the name of your father and mother. Be careful and not forget your English tongue. If you shall have an opportunity to get away from the Indians, don't try to escape; for if you do, they will find and destroy you. Don't forget, my little daughter, the prayers that I have learned you—and say them often; be a good child, and God will bless you. May God bless you my child and make you comfortable and happy.*[63]

The Indians killed and scalped everyone they had taken captive with the exception of Mary and the little boy. The next morning, Mary, seeing what had occurred, described the bodies of her fellow captives as horribly mangled. She and the boy were then moved by the Indians, leaving the bodies where they lay. Later, when they stopped for the night, Mary observed the Indians taking scalps out of their bags. The scalps were put on stretchers and placed by the fire to dry. Once dry, the Indians scraped the flesh off the scalps to make them ready for market. Mary recognized the scalps as those of her family by the color of their hair; her mother's hair was red. She bore what she witnessed without saying a word. This was only the beginning of what she would withstand on her journey of adoption, assimilation and washing out the white.

After a period of time, Mary Jemison was adopted by Seneca Indians. Eventually, she was married twice, first to a Delaware Indian who later died and then a Seneca Indian. She never returned to the white community, saying that she didn't want to leave her children.

It is likely that Mary Jemison stayed occasionally at a Seneca campground along the Allegheny River in Warren, Pennsylvania. Eventually, she became known as the "Old White Woman of the Genesee." Today, a statue in her honor stands in Adams County, Pennsylvania.

12.

Into the Pennsylvania Wilds

Marie LeRoy, Barbara Leininger and Barbara Hicks

This region, the Pennsylvania Wilds, played a role in the taking of captives. Marie LeRoy and Barbara Leininger, who were taken captive at the Penn's Creek Massacre, spoke about traveling across Pennsylvania before eventually arriving in Kittanning, Armstrong County, just miles from today's Jefferson County, one of the counties in the Pennsylvania Wilds. Another captive, Barbara Hicks, was taken at the Great Cove Massacre and was also held captive at Kittanning.

In their trek with captives, the Indians followed many trails, but with Marie LeRoy and Barbara Leininger, they followed the Great Shamokin Path westward toward Kittanning. Kittanning was the place where Shingas, the chief of the Delaware, and Tewea, also known as Captain Jacob, had villages located on each side of the river. The Great Shamokin Path is one of the oldest paths between the Susquehanna and Ohio, and it follows the West Branch of the Susquehanna River, Bald Eagle Creek, and Marsh Creek, through Clearfield and Punxsutawney.[64]

Eventually, after leaving the Penn's Creek area, the Indians involved in the raid divided into two groups; one went in the direction of the Ohio River, while the other, which included an Indian known as Galasko and captives LeRoy and Leininger, went on to Jenkiklamuhs, a Delaware town on the West Branch of the Susquehanna River (also known as Chinklacamoose, today, it is known as the town of Clearfield in the Pennsylvania Wilds), where they stayed for ten days.[65] There is no written record of the path over which

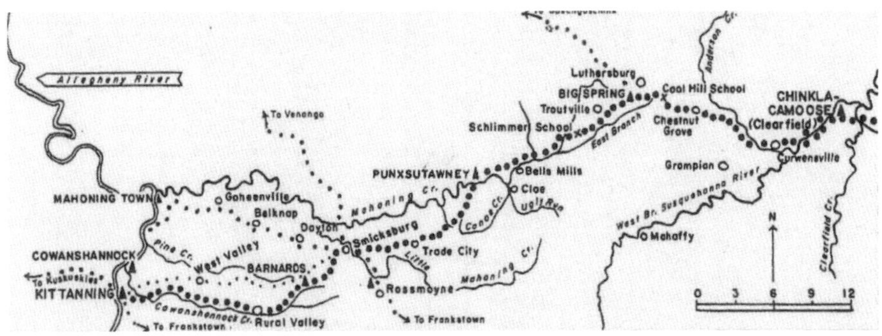

A map of the Great Shamokin Path, as it appears in *Indian Paths of Pennsylvania, by Paul A. W. Wallace. Courtesy of Pennsylvania Historic and Museum Commission, Harrisburg, Pennsylvania.*

Barbara Hicks was taken into the Wilds, but if she traveled the same route as LeRoy and Leininger, it was an arduous journey.

The trip west from Clearfield was not an easy one. As related in an earlier chapter, "Between Chinklacamoose and the mouth of Anderson Creek (Curwensville), several crossings of the Susquehanna were made necessary… in order to escape the high laurel bushes which were a nightmare to travel."[66] Another early account of travel in that region said, "They left the West Branch and traveled 'three miles to the northwest up the creek, crossing it five times.' Here, the path went precipitately up the mountain."[67]

The destination of the Indians and the girls that required them to climb the path that went up the mountain was Ponks-uteney (Punxsutawney, today known as the "Weather Capital of the World"), which, in the Delaware language, means "gnat town," where they rested for five days.[68] One can only wonder what kind of "rest" they experienced there. Punxsutawney, or Gnat Town, was described by John Heckewelder, the Moravian missionary as "a place that was infested with these gnats or sand flies. Not a moment's rest was to be expected at this place otherwise than by kindling fires throughout the camp and sitting in the smoke."[69]

> *In the evening, the ponkis were excessively annoying so that the cattle pressed towards and into our camp to escape their persecutors in the smoke of the fires. This vermin is a plague to man and beast, both by day and night. But, in the swamp, through which we were now passing, their name is legion, and hence the Indians call it Ponksutenik., i.e., "the town of the Ponkis."*[70]

Interestingly, locals today refer to Punxsutawney as Punxsy.

Above: Great Shamokin Path Historic Marker, Clinton County, a Pennsylvania Historic and Museum commission, Harrisburg, Pennsylvania. *Photograph by Ruhrfisch.*

Right: Kittanning Historic Marker. *Courtesy of Larry Small, member of the Armstrong County Historical and Genealogical Society.*

Eventually, LeRoy and Leininger arrived in Kittanning, where Barbara Hicks, who had been taken captive with her four sons at the Tonoloways near the Big Cove, was also being held. There is no evidence that Barbara's sons were with her.

Ten months after the attacks that made these three women captives, Lieutenant Colonel John Armstrong launched an assault on the Indian village of Kittanning in the early morning hours of September 8. The raid resulted in Armstrong regaining eleven captives; one of them was Barbara Hicks. With the town destroyed, the Indians took the rest of the captives farther west into the wilderness. Captain Jacobs (Tewa), who had taken William and Elizabeth Fleming captive at the Great Cove Massacre, was killed in the raid. Armstrong and his men claimed eleven scalps and also claimed the scalp bounty that had been placed on Captain Jacob's head, $350 (this estimate was apparently made using U.S. dollars, which did not exist at the time). Shingas was not present in Kittanning during the attack. The raid aggravated the war and the Indians' response to it.

On, September 23, 1756, the *Pennsylvania Gazette* listed the name of Barbara Hicks as one of the English prisoners who had been saved during Armstrong's Kittanning raid. One historian suggested that Barbara Hicks eventually returned to her home in the Tonolloways (Great Cove area), where she "managed to hold her husband's property for eight years before her children finally returned."[71] With her sons in captivity for approximately six years, it is doubtful that she could have reestablished her former home on her own. Further:

> *Shortly after the raid on November 1, 1755, another attack took place in the area of the Coves. On January 28, 1756, James Leaton was killed and scalped. Catherine Stillwell and one of her children were killed and scalped and two others carried off; one about eight, the other three years old...Samuel Hicks had eleven cattle and a valuable mare killed...a house was burnt that belonged to one Hicks* [John Hicks], *who had been murdered some time ago.*[72]

According to the estate laws of the day, Barbara Hicks would not have inherited the property from her dead husband; rather, her sons would have. A check with the Pennsylvania Archives for property ownership listed under the name of John Hicks from 1733 to 1780 in the patent land records and land warrant records from 1733 to 1957 revealed no land records for John Hicks/Hick/Heck/Hix. This leads to the conclusion the Hicks family were squatters on their Pennsylvania land—as many were at that time—or if the land was purchased, a deed to the property was never filed. Nothing further is known of Barbara Hicks.

Marie LeRoy and Barbara Leininger, who had been held at Kittanning with Barbara Hicks, were among those who were taken farther into the interior by the Indians. Within their narrative, they described the fate of a woman who had escaped with Armstrong but was recaptured:

> *First, they scalped her; next, they laid burning splinters of wood, here and there, upon her body; and then they cut off her ears and fingers, forcing them into her mouth so that she had to swallow them. Amidst such torments, this woman lived from nine o'clock in the morning until toward sunset, when a French officer took compassion on her, and put her out of her misery. An English soldier, on the contrary, named John, who escaped from prison at Lancaster, and joined the French, had a piece of flesh cut from her body, and ate it. When she was dead, the Indians chopped her in two, through the middle, and let her lie until the dogs came and devoured her.*[73]

The narrative continued:

> *Three days later, an Englishman was brought in, who had, likewise, attempted to escape with Col. Armstrong, and burned alive in the same village. His torments, however, continued only about three hours; but his screams were frightful to listen to. It rained that day very hard, so that the Indians could not keep up the fire. Hence, they began to discharge gunpowder into his body. At last, amidst his worst pains, when the poor man called for a drink of water, they brought him melted lead, and poured it down his throat. This draught at once helped him out of the hands of the barbarians, for he died on the instant.*[74]

What psychological terror took place in the minds of the captives who viewed these atrocities? Not only had they been dragged away from civilization, they then faced the reality of what would happen to them if they didn't conform or attempted to escape.

To their good fortune, Marie LeRoy and Barbara Leininger eventually escaped captivity.

> *Early in 1759, at least two escape plots were hatching among captives of the Delaware held on the West Branch of the Muskingum* [Ohio]. *These coalesced into a single plan to free Barbara Leininger, Marie LeRoy, Hugh "Owen" Gibson and recently arrived David Brackenridge. After gathering a bit of food stored by other plotters and feigning serious illness to allow separation from the village, the four skirted settlements along the river, rafted across, and then ran for nearly twenty-four hours. Gibson, who was handy with the gun he brought sustained them by killing two deer. The group traveled four days, and about 100 miles, to reach the Ohio River. After crossing the river, they traveled east for a week, arriving at Fort Pitt after sixteen days. The escapees were in good enough condition to resume traveling eastward the next day.*[75]

The long journey of the two girls, who started in eastern Pennsylvania and traveled and camped in Pennsylvania Wilds as captives of the Indians, ended after four years.

In the years following her captivity, it is recorded that Marie LeRoy married her cousin Adam LeRoy. Adam LeRoy, at one point, went back to Switzerland to claim property that belonged to Marie's father, John Jacob LeRoy. The steward in charge of the property turned over 1,379 crowns to Adam LeRoy. As the story goes, any money that was taken out of the country was subject to a tax. In order to avoid the tax, LeRoy converted the money into Sweitzer cheese and brought it to Philadelphia, where he sold it, receiving an amount equal to what had been left in trust in Switzerland.[76] Marie LeRoy's brother, John James LeRoy, settled in Prince George's County, Maryland. Neither Marie nor her brother ever returned to the scene of the Penn's Valley Massacre. Marie died in Lancaster in 1800.[77]

According to descendants of Barbara Leininger, she married Peter Ruffner at Trinity Lutheran Church in New Holland, Lancaster, Pennsylvania, on February 1, 1761. They were the parents of three known children.[78]

13.
WHITE INDIANS

When I first learned the term *White Indian*, I assumed it was referring to captives who were so converted to Indian ways that they joined the Indians in their attacks on the settlers. Well, this is both true and untrue. Captives were a mixed group of very young children, teens and adults, and there were both male and female captives. Certainly, captive Mary Jemison, a White Indian, was not raiding, nor were Marie LeRoy or Barbara Leininger.

James Axtell, the author of *The White Indians of Colonial America* (1975), asked the question, "If you were a 'white' prisoner of Native Americans, would you have escaped back to your culture or remained as an Indian?" This is a powerful question when you realize what the captives witnessed and were subject to. In light of the modern term Stockholm syndrome, what can be made of the phenomenon of White Indians? According to an article by Laura Lambert, which was posted by the *Encyclopedia Britannica*:

> *Stockholm syndrome* [is a] *psychological response wherein a captive begins to identify closely with his or her captors, as well as with their agenda and demands.*
>
> *Psychologists who have studied the syndrome believe that the bond is initially created when a captor threatens a captive's life, deliberates and then chooses not to kill the captive. The captive's relief at the removal of the threat of death is transposed into feelings of gratitude toward the captor for giving them their life. As the Stockholm bank robbery (committed in 1973*

and involving the taking of captives) incident proved, it takes only a few days for this bond to cement, proving that, early on, the victim's desire to survive trumps the urge to hate the person who created the situation.[79]

James Smith

James Smith, a famous Pennsylvania captive, wrote of his encounters with the Indians between 1755 and 1759 some forty-four years after his escape. He did not make clear whether he participated in Indian raiding parties during his years in captivity.

Adoption was a common practice among the Indians; a captive would be given to someone who had lost a loved one. In James Smith's account, he detailed his experience of being forced to "run the gauntlet" and the process of adoption.

Smith was captured in May 1755, while working on a road near Bedford. Unaware of any danger, as he was traveling with a companion, Smith was attacked by three Indians who were hiding behind a blind. Smith's companion was shot and scalped. Smith was taken captive. Forced to run across Pennsylvania, Smith and his captors reached Fort Duquesne after several days. As they approached the fort, he heard shouts from the Indians and thought there must have been thousands of them, which was not the case.

Seeing Indians dressed in breech cloth and moccasins running toward him, Smith thought he would be killed. Instead, the Indians formed two lines. Smith was forced to run between them while they struck him with switches, hatchets or their fists, a practice known as running the gauntlet. After Smith was knocked to the ground, unconscious, the next thing he remembered was waking up in the fort and being tended to by a French physician.

After a period of recuperation, Smith was taken to a town in the Ohio. When he arrived, Indians gathered around him. One began pulling the hair out of his head by dipping his fingers in ashes in order to take a firmer hold of it. The Indian pulled until all of the hair was out of Smith's head except for a small spot, about three or four square inches on the crown. This remaining hair was trimmed, and two locks were wrapped with a narrow beaded band, and the other was "plaited" down its full length and adorned with silver. Next, his ears and nose were pierced, and he was given jewelry for each. Following this, Smith was ordered to strip and put on a breechcloth. His body was painted with several colors, and a large belt of wampum was put around his neck and silver bands on his hands and arms. The old chief then took him into the center of the village and gave out the halloo alarm, which brought the town of Indians running. The chief held Smith's hand and made a long speech. At the end of the speech, he gave Smith to three young squaws, who took him to the bank of the river.

Sure that he was going to be drowned, Smith resisted until one of the squaws who could speak some English told him, "No hurt you." He was then dunked in the water and washed. When he came out, he was taken to the council house, where he was given new clothes and moccasins, again painted and then presented with a pipe and tomahawk. The chief noted that he was then of their flesh and that all of his whiteness had been washed out of his blood. So, James Smith became an adoptive of an Indian tribe.[80]

James Smith escaped captivity in 1759 and resided in Conococheague Valley, Pennsylvania, where he became a farmer and married Anne Wilson in 1763. In 1764, he joined Colonel Bouquet in his expedition to the Muskingum River to return the captives. Smith represented Westmoreland County, Pennsylvania, at the Constitutional Convention in 1776, and he joined the Pennsylvania militia as a captain during the Revolutionary War, eventually achieving the rank of colonel. After his first wife died in 1778, he moved to Westmoreland County, where he remarried. In later years, he and his family settled in Bourbon County, Kentucky.

Gershom Hicks

There is an unmarked grave somewhere near Warren, Pennsylvania (most likely in Brokenstraw Township), where the remains of a man who was instrumental in opening up the Wilds region and one of its early settlers is buried. His name was Gershom Hicks. In the Bible, Gershom was the name of the son of Moses. The name is descriptive of one who is an exile, alien, foreign or, as the Bible speaks of the children of Israel in the wilderness, "sojourner there." Gershom Hicks's parents could not have chosen a more evocative name for their son, as he experienced a tragic event that changed his life forever.

Taken captive in 1755 in the area known as the Great Cove and Tonoloway (Conolloway), Hicks and his brothers witnessed the trauma of the attack that led to the deaths of their brother and father. Unlike others, they were not murdered on the trail but survived. With no written narrative from this family, based on the surviving narratives of others, it is certain they endured the ordeal of the gauntlet that was described by James Smith.

In historical accounts, Hicks has been described by the British as a White Indian, a villain and a rascal. But in witnessing the atrocities of these attacks, the survival instinct would have kicked in quickly. Did he and his brothers believe they would never return to white society? What actions did they take to survive?

Gershom was the oldest brother, the year of his birth given as approximately 1734, which would have made him about twenty-one years old when he was captured. It is possible to envision a scenario in which the brothers were kept together, with Gershom watching over the younger ones. If there had been chances for escape, it is conceivable that he didn't act on the opportunity in order to stay near his younger siblings. Held captive for approximately six years, there is evidence that, after their return from captivity, Gershom, Levi and Moses Hicks lived very near to one another.

Through the period of their captivity, there was no recorded report of the Hicks brothers. One small bit of information about Gershom's time of captivity did come to light in the writings of John Adlum, the author of "Communications of the Cultivation of the Vine," which was published in a newspaper in 1820, long after Gershom Hicks's return to the White world. Adlum met Hicks in 1790, when he and Samuel Maclay were touring the West Branch of the Susquehanna, Sinnemahoning and Allegheny Rivers, where Gershom Hicks acted as one of their guides. The article quotes Adlum's conversation with Hicks regarding his first captivity.

> *Gershom Hicks, born 1734, was taken prisoner, along with his brothers, Mosses and Levi, the year before General Braddock's defeat* [this reference would put their captivity at 1754, which is in conflict with their actual captive date of 1755]. *Adlum notes that Gershom Hicks said he was taken to the French Creek, where every fall, the prisoners, boys and girls, went to Presque Isle to gather grapes for the French officers at that garrison, which grew in considerable quantities on the peninsula. The French soldiers treaded "them* [the grapes] *with their feet, in a vat, and he saw them press out the wine and fill a number of casks." This was "repeated as long as the French held that post. The presumption is that if the wine had not been pretty good, they would not have continued the practice."*[81]

After six years in captivity, sometime around 1761, Gershom Hicks appeared in the historical record with Patrick Allison, an Indian trader.

Hicks was described as his servant. In an article published in the *Western Pennsylvania Historical Magazine* 17, no. 3, in September 1934, Gershom Hicks was listed as a fur trader in the Upper Ohio Valley who was considered to be less than honorable. In fact, the author of the article claimed that many of the traders were disreputable; Benjamin Franklin also made this claim, although the writer did admit it was a tough business and that when the traders ventured into Indian territory, they never knew if they would come back. Allison was not named in the list; however, if he and Hicks had been working together in the Ohio Valley, Gershom's knowledge of the region would have made him a valuable asset.

Hicks's Indian skills were similarly not lost on the British military. Around 1761, "Gershom was also hired as a guide by the British commander at Fort Venango, who called him 'a fellow who has been prisoner with the Indians and just the same as one of themselves.'"[82]

The Girty Brothers

The Girty brothers were other examples of White Indians. The children of an Indian trader who was known to have traded with the Delaware, the Girty children were familiar with the language and culture of the Indians. They shared a similar captive story with the Hicks family, as their entire family was taken. Their mother, Mary Girty-Turner, was remarried, and the family included Mary; her infant son; John Turner, her second husband of two years; and her four sons with Girty, James, Simon, George and Thomas, and they were all captured at the fall of Fort Granville in 1756. Three weeks after witnessing his stepfather's torture and death, Thomas Girty was retaken when Armstrong launched his attack on the Delaware villages at Kittanning. The Girty family was dispersed by the Indians, with Mary and her baby sent to a Shawnee town; twelve-year-old James adopted into another tribe; fifteen-year-old Simon adopted by the Western Seneca; and ten-year-old George adopted by the Delaware. James, Simon and George remained among the Indians for nearly eight years. They were returned in the release of captives in 1764 and 1765.[83]

Simon Girty moved back and forth between white and Indian society, working as a translator, messenger and spy. In the Revolutionary War, Simon Girty, like James Smith and Gershom Hicks, joined the colonials in the fight against the British. But Simon, with strong feelings for the Indians he had been with for so long, reversed sides and defected to the British in 1778. He went on to work for the British as an interpreter and remained on the British Indian department's payroll as a diplomat, spy and soldier for the next forty years. He married another Indian captive, Catherine Malott, and they relocated to Canada, where they raised three children.[84]

One Girty brother, George, apparently returned to the Delaware after his release, marrying and raising a family. All three "Indian Girtys" were recognized and feared as White Indians.[85]

14.

An Incident at Fort Pitt

Eighteenth-Century Germ Warfare

In May 1763, during Pontiac's Rebellion, the Indians began a siege of Fort Pitt. By June, the hostilities had increased, and a Swiss-born captain by the name of Simeon Ecuyer reported to his superior, Colonel Bouquet, who was, at that time, in Philadelphia, the seriousness of the situation. The Indians had burned nearby houses in an attempt to draw the force out of the well-defended fort to fight them. The fort was providing refuge to colonists, traders and those who were trespassing on Indian lands. But information on the conditions in the fort caught the attention of Colonel Bouquet. Ecuyer reported, "We are so crowded in the fort that I fear disease, for, in spite of all my care, I cannot keep the place as clean as I should like; moreover, the small pox is among us. For this reason, I have had a hospital built under the bridge beyond musket-fire."[86]

Smallpox is an insidious disease that had its origin thousands of years ago. According to the CDC, its origin is unknown, but smallpox is believed to have begun causing illness and deaths as early as the third century BCE in the Egyptian empire. Its early symptoms are high fever, head and body aches and sometimes vomiting. The disease progresses from these early symptoms to red spots in the mouth and tongue. These sores, in turn, break down in the mouth, and soon, a rash appears on the skin. The sores fill with an opaque fluid, and the ill person's temperature rises again. Four weeks after the rash appears, the scabs have fallen off; however, the disease leaves permanent scars.[87] The Indian population had no immunity to this disease,

An unnamed artist's interpretation of Fort Pitt in 1759 with the Allegheny (*left*) and Monongahela Rivers (*right*). At their confluence is the Ohio River (*bottom*). *Courtesy of Wikimedia Commons.*

which traveled across the globe to the Americas, and it was particularly devastating to those people.

Henry Bouquet, who received the information on the smallpox outbreak at Fort Pitt, was born in 1719 in Switzerland, and at seventeen years of age, he entered the military. A professional soldier, Bouquet made his rounds in the militaries of several countries and eventually entered the British Army in 1754 as a lieutenant colonel in the Sixtieth Regiment of Foot, a unit made up largely of members of Pennsylvania's German immigrant community. In 1758, he was ordered to take part in Forbes's expedition against Fort Duquesne, which was once held by the French but deserted at the time.

Eventually, Bouquet was drawn into Pontiac's Rebellion (1763–1764). While the French and Indian War had ended with the Treaty of Paris in 1763, the frontier of Pennsylvania was embroiled in this new conflict as Chief Pontiac, dissatisfied over the British defeat of the French and Britain's ultimate control of the Ohio Valley, rallied the Indians to join him.

It was during this time that Gershom and Levi Hicks, who had been taken captive by the Delaware Indians in 1755 at the Great Cove Massacre, arrived on the scene at Fort Pitt. Both came out of captivity around 1761and worked for Indian traders. It appears they had been taken prisoner by the Indians again in 1763, during Pontiac's Rebellion.

Oil painting, *Colonel Henry Bouquet, circa 1759–60,* by John Wollaston, Philadelphia History Museum. *Courtesy of Wikimedia Commons.*

I first read about the adventures of the "mysterious Hicks brothers," as one writer referred to them, in a series of newspaper articles that were published in Pennsylvania newspapers over a period of time. These articles were based on "Rung's Chronicles of Pennsylvania History," a series of historical articles by Albert M. Rung that were published by the Huntingdon County Historical Society between 1951 and 1957 and in the *Daily News* (Huntingdon, Pennsylvania). According to Rung, the information related in these articles was based on *The Papers of Col. Henry Bouquet,* which was compiled from Bouquet's correspondence that was housed in the British Museum and the Library of Congress. Rung stated that "a number of volumes with paper covers and mimeographed pages made their appearance in 1942, along with their title page including, 'Prepared by Pennsylvania Historical Survey… edited by Sylvester K. Stevens and Donald H. Kent, Commonwealth of Pennsylvania, Department of Public Instruction, Pennsylvania Historical Commission, Harrisburg, 1942.'"[88]

When Gershom Hicks arrived at Fort Pitt in 1764, it had been nearly a year since a smallpox outbreak had taken place among the Indians in 1763. Almost immediately, Hicks, who had acted as a guide for the British in 1761, was immediately under suspicion of being an Indian spy. On April 27, 1764, Lieutenant Theodor Friedrich Winter at Fort Pitt sent a message to Colonel Bouquet, who was at Carlisle. It read, "Some days ago, one Hicks, an Englishman, came in from the Indians and has given a long history, which Capt. Grant sends you by this Express."[89] Another correspondence from Captain John Steward, in his communication to Bouquet the next day, said:

> *Ligonier 27th April 1764. 12 o'clock at Night. Sir, Inclosed* [sic] *I send you the returns from Capt. Grant, who writes me that that rascal Hicks, who came into that Post Some time ago, has made a full Confession, which I made no doubt he has Acquainted you of.*[90] *I hope if these villains should attempt this post, I hope we shall be able to give a good account of them, the Express tells me he saw one Indian at Creightons plantation but*

> *believes there might be more, as he saw two horses. I have acquainted the commanding officer at Bedford of everything Capt. Grant has wrote me about those villains; So, I hope every body* [sic] *will be upon their guard.*[91]

Bouquet stated in his reply on May 3, 1764, "It is very lucky that that rascal Hicks has been made to confess his treachery, which confirms the absolute necessity of never trusting an Indian under any form or appearance. As there may be some truth in his prevarications it is very proper to be extremely vigilant to prevent any surprise."[92]

The deposition of Gershom Hicks was taken on April 14, 1764, which was the information forwarded by Captain Grant to Colonel Bouquet:

> *Garshom Hicks, a man of about thirty years of age arrived at Fort Pitt, having made his escape from the Indians, says that he was a servant to Patrick Allison an Indian trader and was made prisoner last May by the Shawneese near Muskingum the rest of his fellow horse drivers, four in number, being killed by the Savages about the same time; the Shawneese kept him prisoner about four days then gave him to a Delaware known by the name of Capt. Bullet who kept him near twenty days at a place called Moquesin, a Delaware town on Muskingum River, from thence, he was sent to help build a house at the Salt Licks for White Eyes, a Delaware chief at which place he remained all winter hunting thereabouts for meat for himself and some other white prisoners that were with the Delawares at that place. /vizt: John Gibson & one Morris/ That about thirty Day agoe* [sic] *he was sent to a place called Hockhockin, where King Beaver lives at present about thirdy* [sic] *miles on this side the Sioto, where he was to hunt in company with two Delawares, that in a few days one of them left him and went home again to go to war leaving orders with Hicks to follow him, which he did in eight or nine days afterwards and went up the Hockhocking River for near a mile, leaving the other Indian by himself to hunt, that he thought this a good time to come off, so turned back again with his cannoe* [sic] *and came into the Ohio River into which the Hockhocking River empty's itself, then crossed the Ohio to the southeast side when he left his cannoe* [sic] *and came up by land having his gun and about twenty loads of powder and ball with him. Says this is eight days agoe* [sic] *and that he saw the Indians the day before yesterday, making a raft to cross the river to the side he was on about 100 miles below this fort. He further says there was a council held at the Salt Licks last fall by the Delawares, in which it was agreed that*

> *two of their chiefs with White Eyes should be sent to some of the French forts on the Mississippi, who, accordingly, went to ask the French to join them to make war against the English this spring and to give them some ammunition, which article he says he is very sure neither the Shawneese or Delawares have above a pint and many of them but half a pint of powder each man and lead in proportion.*[93]

There was a note added to the deposition that Hicks spoke the Delaware language very well and that he understood the Shawnee tongue a little.

As Hicks's deposition continued, he stated that the Indians had great confidence in him from his being a prisoner once before and that he had "friends amongst them, and therefore trusted with all their 'secrets and designs.'"[94]

> *He further says that White Eyes and the two other chiefs returned again the beginning of last March very much dissatisfied with the answers they got from the French....That they were all as one with the English now and wou'd* [sic] *not fight against them.*
>
> *Hicks says he thinks that, with the Delawares and Shawnese, he had seen about 50 or 60 white prisoners most of which are women and young persons and most of them taken last war* [French and Indian War]*; that the small pox has been very general and raging amongst the Indians since last spring and that 30 or 40 Mingoes, as many Delawares and some Shawneese died all of the small pox since that time, that it still continues amongst them.*[95]

The British did not place much credibility in his statements, and he was closely watched inside the fort. Why was this deposition, in which Hicks gave information about the Indians' plans, their numbers and the interactions between tribes, under suspicion? Could it have had something to do with his mention of smallpox, which had been raging among the Indians since the prior spring?

General Jeffrey Amherst, Bouquet's commander, discussed an idea to infect the Indians near Fort Pitt with smallpox by giving them infected blankets from the fort's smallpox hospital. Amherst, who was known for his contempt of the Indians, wrote to Bouquet, who was in Lancaster on June 29, 1763, asking if such a plan could be carried out. "Could it not be contrived to send small pox among those disaffected tribes of Indians? We must, on this occasion, use every stratagem in our power to reduce them."[96] Bouquet agreed to carry out the plan himself. Amherst suggested the smallpox blanket method or any other method Bouquet could use to rid them of the Indians.

The commander of the militia at the fort, William Trent, provided additional information on the plan:

> [June] *24th* [1763] *The Turtles Heart, a principal Warrior of the Delawares and Mamaltee, a Chief, came within a small distance of the fort. Mr. Mckee went out to them, and they made a speech letting us know that all our* [posts] *as Ligonier was destroyed, that great numbers of Indians* [were coming and] *that, out of regard to us, they had prevailed on 6 Nations* [not to] *attack us but give us time to go down the country and they desired we would set off immediately. The commanding officer thanked them, let them know that we had everything we wanted, that we could defend it against all the Indians in the woods, that we had three large armys* [sic] *marching to chastise those Indians that had struck us, told them to take care of their women and children, but not to tell any other Indians, they said they would go and speak to their chiefs and come and tell us what they said, they returned and said they would hold fast of the chain of friendship. Out of our regard to them, we gave them two blankets and an handkerchief out of the small pox hospital. I hope it will have the desired effect. They then told us that Ligonier had been attacked, but that the enemy were beat.*[97]

It is not known who proposed the smallpox plan to Trent or who physically gave the Indians the blankets, but the records for that date at Fort Pitt show the following entries:

> *To sundries got to replace in kind those which were taken from people in the hospital to convey the smallpox to the Indians Viz:*
> *2 Blankets at 20/£299 09 0*
> *1 silk handkerchef 10/&1 linnen do: 3/6 099 1399 6*[98]

Hicks's arrival at Fort Pitt and his story about smallpox has been studied by a number of scientists. One scientist, Elizabeth A. Fenn, an assistant professor of history of George Washington University, wrote about biological warfare in eighteenth-century North America. In those writings, she suggests that there may have been more than one plan to send smallpox to the Indians and that the exchange of blankets was not necessarily the Amherst plan. She notes that, in the deposition of Gershom Hicks, Hicks speaks of the outbreak of smallpox among the Indians that he had observed. In her studies, Fenn believes that the Fort Pitt episode, generally treated as an anomaly, points out that biological warfare may have been used more extensively than has been believed.[99]

Others say it was impossible to infect the Indians with blankets from the smallpox ward. In a discussion about how long the smallpox virus can survive, it was found that if the blankets had been kept in a wooden box, the virus could have survived for a lengthy period of time. But if the blankets had been in the open, the rate of survival would not have been as great. One scientist, however, has stated that the virus could have remained viable at room temperature or its equivalent for two to three weeks. Since the blankets were given to the Indians in June, would it have been warm enough for the virus to remain viable? If the Indians who had received the blankets and the handkerchief had distributed those infected items to other Indians who were living in close proximity to the fort, is it possible that a few Indians there could have contracted the virus? Smallpox has a seven- to seventeen-day incubation period. As the Indians were known to travel great distances, could the virus have been spread from Fort Pitt to the Indians in the Ohio Valley?

There is another point to be made in this conversation about the smallpox outbreak. It seems to be a fact that the British at Fort Pitt seeded the blankets. When Gershom Hicks arrived at the fort and disclosed what he had seen of the outbreak of smallpox among the Indians, it's possible that the eighteenth-century British officers would not have had extensive knowledge about the transmission rate of the virus and how long it took to spread. They may have concluded the outbreak was their doing, whether or not the virus survived long enough to infect those Indians in the Ohio Valley. In other words, when Hicks arrived with his story at the fort, they were guilty of the act of having given out smallpox seeded blankets and did not want direct eye-witness testimony to magnify their act of germ warfare. What better way to keep their deed quiet than to cast suspicion on the man who made the report?

Over a period of time, Hicks was reexamined and threatened with execution. Although his story changed several times, his last testimony began by stating that he had left Hockhockin about thirty days earlier with seven Delaware Indians to go to war with the frontier inhabitants. They passed English forts from a distance until they came to Shareman's Valley, where they murdered James Evens and his wife and made prisoners of two boys who were about eight and twelve years old. When they drew near Fort Pitt, the Indians urged Hicks to go to the fort and say he had escaped. In that way, he was to try to learn what provisions, ammunition and troops were at the fort and what guards were kept on duty and other observations. He was told to return to them in two days with the information, and if he couldn't return in that time, he was to follow them when he could, as the Indians were moving on with the two captive boys.[100]

Following this "confession," the soldiers arrested him and showed him the place where they intended to execute him by hanging. In the morning, after being taken to the crudely constructed gallows, Hicks, standing under it, was thoroughly terrified and begged for mercy. Relating additional information to the officers regarding the activities of two Delaware Chiefs the previous winter, he also reported on the condition of the Indians through the winter and said that the French traders were to supply them with ammunition.

It was at this juncture that Levi Hicks, the brother of Gershom, arrived at the fort. Levi was also described by the British as a "most notorious offender." But he was also someone who could corroborate the intelligence Gershom Hicks had provided, intelligence that Bouquet would need to attack the Indians.

Bouquet, who had been made commander of Fort Pitt, was moving to subdue the Indians. On his way to Fort Pitt, the notification reached him that Levi Hicks had arrived, and the reply came.

> *Fort Bedford, September 10, 1764. Yesterday, Colonel Bouquet marched from hence with a large convoy of provisions and ammunition, on pack-horses, for Fort Pitt, and lay last night at the Shawanese Cabbins* [sic]—*To-morrow, a convoy of 60 or 70 waggons* [sic] *is to follow, under the command of Captain Hay, of the royal artillery—And the next day, the last convoy of pack-horses, under the Command of Captain Ourry, with the rear of the troops.*
>
> *It is hoped that these covoys will all get up with very little difficulty, as Captain Williams, cheief* [sic] *engineer, precedes them with workmen to repair the roads. He has, with 200 Pennsylvanians, completed, in four days, a most excellent waggon* [sic] *road round the sidling hill. A number of volunteers from Virginia are on their march to join the army at Ft. Pitt.*[101]

15.

Return of the Captives

While Pontiac's Rebellion raged across the frontier, the conflict ended in 1764, when Bouquet led a successful expedition from Fort Pitt to the Muskingum River, where hundreds of captives were being held in the Ohio. With peace established, many of the captives who had been taken over the years were returned.

The Hicks brothers remained prisoners at Fort Pitt. Did the information supplied by them lead to Bouquet's successful expedition? Possibly. Bouquet's careful planning resulted in the suppression of the Indians and was accomplished without bloodshed.

From New York, an account of Bouquet's journey into the Ohio was published:

> *New York, November 15. By the following letter, we have a further account of the progress of the army under the command of Colonel Bouquet.*
>
> *From the Camp near Tuscarawas, October 20, "Our little army reached this place after a march of ten days without halting, thro' a hilly country, and many streams to pass, which gave some interruption to our pack-horses: the savages terrified, and astonished to find their woods will not protect them, are coming in the most abject manner, to beg our mercy, and ask for peace, or they must immediately flyaway, and abandon their country. We have had some meetings with their chiefs, wherein our commander upbraided them in severe terms for their cruelties and treachery; and, particularly, for their late perfidious behavior, in amusing our forces on Lake Erie, with a*

> *fallacious peace, and the notorious lye* [sic] *that they had recalled their murderers from our frontiers, whilst their parties were committing the most cruel murders, and continued their massacres almost to this time. They acknowledged every thing* [sic] *and begged mercy and foregiveness* [sic]*; where they are to bring in all their prisoners to be delivered up, and there, it is said, we shall make peace with them."*[102]

While part of the peace settlement was the return of captives, the Indians were reluctant to return them and had great feelings about releasing those they had "adopted" and considered to be members of their families. In the end, about three hundred captives returned to Pittsburgh with a victorious Bouquet. During the winter of 1764–65, British agents traveled throughout the Ohio villages, discovering remaining captives. Between Bouquet's advance in Muskingum in the fall of 1764 and the summer of 1765, over five hundred captives had been returned to the British at Fort Pitt.[103] The return of captives was a slow process. More than one thousand captives were not returned and were never heard from again.[104]

Those who were returned were never entirely free; the "red colonials" faced suspicions, expectations and challenges.[105] Alan Fitzpatrick, the author of a book titled *The White Indians*, spoke at the Ohio County Public Library in 2016, and he discussed the reasons white captives may not have come home after peace was made with the Natives. His theory was:

> *It was an empowering way of life* [for the whites with the Indians]. *It* [Indian society] *valued every individual in a classless society. That's why they didn't come back….It's too easy for us to make judgments about them from a 21st-century perspective…18th-century colonial life was very, very class-structured with a vertical structure of gentry, aristocrats, magistrates, military tradesmen, farmers, slaves and indentured servants. There was no upward movement. In this class structure, land was everything; land ownership was everything. Land was owned by the upper class.*[106]

Reading an advertisement from February 1765 shines further light on the sad situation of several children who were returned:

> *NOTICE is hereby given, that six of the captives recovered by Col. Bouquet from the Indians, in November last, are now at Philadelphia, under the care of this government, viz, three boys and three girls, whose descriptions are respectively as follows:*

Painting, *The Indians Delivering Up the English Captives to Colonel Bouquet*, by Benjamin West. *Courtesy of the Library of Congress.*

BOYS. Stephen, about 14 years old, fair complexion, and light brown hair, and dark brown eyes. William, about 12 years of age, brown complexion, black hair and black eyes. The other boy, name unknown, about the same age, fair complexion, brown hair, and brown eyes.

GIRLS. Betty, sister to William, about 9 years of age, dark complexion, black eyes, and black hair. Rachel, about 10 years of age, fair complexion, grey eyes, and light brown hair. Catherine, about 9 years old, fair complexion, light brown eyes, and brown hair.

They have been several years among the Indians, and do not recollect their surnames, nor from what place they were taken.

Such persons therefore as have had their children or other relations carried into captivity during the first Indian war, upon application to the provincial commissioners in this city, within six weeks, may see the above mentioned children, and if they find any of their relations among them, are requested to take them away, otherwise the boys will be bound out to trades, and the girls so disposed of, that they may be no further expence [sic] *to the publick* [sic].[107]

One of the most poignant stories of returned captives involved the sister of Barbara Leininger, Regina. The ten-year-old was taken captive during the Penn Creek Massacre of 1755 along with her sister, but later, they were separated. When she was returned to Bouquet's army nine year later, she was unrecognizable. Her mother, searching for her among the redeemed captives at Carlisle, feared she would never find her, as Regina had no identifying marks on her body. Recalling the German hymns she had sung to her children those long years before, Regina's mother began to sing one that would have been familiar to her children. Hearing the words, Regina recognized the song from her childhood and ran to her mother, a joyful reunion.[108]

Shingas, the Delaware chief who was instrumental in so many being taken captive, disappeared from the record in the winter of 1763–64. Some have suggested that he was a victim of the smallpox outbreak that was spreading among the Indians that year. (This was attested to by Hicks, but there is no firm proof.)

The fate of the Hicks brothers was left to the civil authorities. On December 1, 1764, Bouquet issued an order to Colonel Asher Clayton at Fort Pitt to march the Hicks brothers to Carlisle, where they were to be held until the governor gave orders for their trial. There is no record that the brothers were ever tried by the civil court. Did the civil authorities view their actions in a different light than the military? Their valuable information led, in part, to Bouquet's successful expedition and the return of hundreds of captives who had been held for years. Gershom and Levi Hicks may very well have laid the groundwork for Bouquet's victory.

Did the Hicks brothers, who were apparently out of captivity in 1761 (when both were servants to Indian traders), only to be captured again in

1763, really go back to raiding with the Indians, or did Gershom Hicks tell the officers what they wanted to hear? Did their recapture by the Indians resurrect Stockholm Syndrome, and did their survival instincts once again take hold of their minds? These are questions that remain unanswered.

James Smith, one of the most famous White Indians, was held for five years as an adopted member of the tribe. He never made clear in his writings whether he took part in raiding parties. Interestingly, White Indian James Smith, who had returned from captivity in 1759, took part in Bouquet's campaign into Ohio with information that was provided by White Indians Gershom and Levi Hicks. White Indians Smith and Gershom Hicks went on to serve in the Continental army during the American Revolution.

16.

Murdered Indians at Stump's Run

On January 16, 1768, a letter sent by express from John Armstrong in Carlisle to the governor described that Frederick Stump and his servant had killed a number of Indians at Stump's Run.

In December 1767, Anglo-Indian relations on Pennsylvania's western frontier were tense. Frontier families continued to settle lands prohibited by treaty. The Pennsylvania Assembly denounced the settlers "audacious encroachments" and began working on a bill for the removal of the settlers. It was in this tense atmosphere, in January 1768, that Frederick Stump and his servant, John Ironcutter, killed four Indian men, three Indian women and three Indian children over a two-day period. The first deaths were those of two Seneca men, their wives and two male Mohicans, with one of the men being scalped. The bodies were then dragged into a nearby creek, breaking the ice as the bodies were pushed in. The next day, Stump and Ironcutter walked fourteen miles to several Indian cabins. Finding a woman and three girls, the men killed them, placed their remains in the cabins and burned the buildings.[109]

On January 23, Captain William Patterson (formerly of Lancaster County but then residing in Juniata) heard of the atrocity, and without waiting for orders from the governor, along with nineteen men, he arrested Stump. Aware of how the relatives of the murdered Indians would receive this news, he sent Gershom Hicks, who apparently had gained the confidence of the government, with a message dated January 22, 1768, to the Indians at Great Island, which was located on the West Branch of the Susquehanna River.

> *Brothers of the Six Nations, Delawares, and other inhabitants of the West Branch of the Susquehanna, hear what I have to say to you—Stump and John Ironcutter, hath, unadvisedly, murdered ten of our friend-Indians near Fort Augusta....Brothers, I being truly sensible of the injury done you, I only add these few words, with my heart's wish, that you may not rashly let go the fast hold of our chain of friendship, for the ill conduct of one of our bad men. Believe me, Brothers, we Englishmen continue the same love for you that usually subsisted between our grandfathers.*[110]

The chief of the Indians at Great Island received Hicks and allowed him to deliver the message. In reply, the chief sent a letter back to Captain William Patterson, dated February 17, 1768:

> *Loving Brother: I received your speech by Gershom Hicks and have sent one of my relations to you with a string of Wampum, and the following answer: Loving Brother: I am glad to hear from you; I understand that you are very much grieved, and that the tears run from your eyes. With both my hands, I now wipe away those tears; and, as I don't doubt but your heart is disturbed. I remove the sorrow from it, and make it as easy as before....As it was the Evil Spirit who caused Stump to commit this bad action, I blame none of my Brothers, the English, but him."*[111]

Hicks and his intercession with the Indians to help them understand the position of the provincial government and, thus, avoid sparking additional conflict is to his credit.

The men responsible for the crime, both imprisoned in Carlisle, were freed by a sympathetic mob before they could be tried. They were never recaptured. Frederick Stump fled to Tennessee, where he settled with a wife.

Part III

THE AMERICAN REVOLUTION

17.

The Great Runaway

Following the years of turmoil that were the French and Indian War and the years that followed under British rule, the colonials had learned one thing: they could take on the British army. The British, who generally looked down on the settlers who served in the army with them, often passed settlers over for promotion in favor of those who were the British regulars. The colonials were prepared to fight.

***

The Pennsylvania and Virginia militia also gave the Indians reason to distrust them. In February 1778, when a body of militia failed to reach their mission of destroying British stores at Cuyahoga, they carried out what was known as the Squaw Campaign, which alienated friendly Delaware. The militia attacked a friendly Delaware camp near present-day New Castle and in Niles, Ohio. Several women and a small boy; the mother of Captain Pipe, an important chief; and Captain Pipe's brother were all killed. This sorry event was precipitated by something simple: heavy rains, which kept the militia from destroying the British stores. It was also responsible for rising sentiments against the Americans.

Initially, during the Revolution, both the Americans and the British advised the Indians not to take sides, a policy that was soon abandoned. In the spring of 1778, there were a number of Tories in the Juniata Valley who were being advised by Tory emissaries from Detroit and Niagara, including Simon Girty, the White Indian mentioned earlier who went among the Indians reminding them of their old grievances.

The Tories concocted a plan to empty the Juniata Valley of its settlers and raise a force of Tories and Indians at Kittanning. The plan involved crossing the mountains, following the Kittanning Trail and eventually breaking into two groups, one to march through the Cove and Conococheague Valleys and the other to follow the Juniata Valley, killing all the settlers in their path before eventually meeting up in Lancaster.

The Tories left their settlements by cover of night; however, unknown to them, they were being watched by an Indian spy known as Captain Logan, who resided in the Juniata Valley at the time and later at Chinklacamoose, now the town of Clearfield. Captain Logan reported the Tories' actions throughout the settlements. With the inhabitants in a state of alarm, Captain Thomas Blair of Path Valley called on all those who wished to fight the Tories, including Indians, to join with him. In forty-eight hours, thirty-five men (volunteers) were ready to fight. At Canoe Valley, they were joined by Gershom and Moses Hicks, who acted as scouts and interpreters.

Captain Blair and his volunteers were successful in destroying and dispersing the Tories. Making their way back home, the men were in high spirits. With night coming on, they built a large fire, and Gershom and Moses Hicks went out to search for game for breakfast. Not anticipating any danger, Gershom shot an elk, and he and Moses skinned and gutted it making preparations to return to camp. Caught off guard, five Indians attacked them and took them as prisoners. After being taken to Detroit, Moses was a prisoner of the Indians for a second time, while Gershom was a prisoner for a third time. How or when Moses Hicks returned from this period of captivity isn't known. Gershom, on the other hand, either escaped or was released from captivity. In 1779, he performed a special espionage mission for General George Washington.

Indian attacks ramped up in Pennsylvania at the time. The Great Runaway, in May 1778, emptied the West Branch Valley of settlers. In a letter to John Hambright of the Supreme Executive Council in Lancaster, Lieutenant Samuel Hunter at Fort Augusta wrote:

> *We are really in a meloncoly* [sic] *situation in this country at present, the back inhabitants* [have] *all evacuated their habitations and assembled in different places....To think what a pannick* [sic] *prevails*

> *in this country; it is really distressing to see the inhabitants flying away and leaving their all.*[112]

By the summer of 1778, Indians from Seneca territory were routinely conducting raids in the Susquehanna Valley. A captured prisoner reported that the Indians planned to kill all the inhabitants on both branches of the river.

18.
Wyoming Valley Massacre

Bolstered by the British, the Indians were seeking to regain the Wyoming Valley, an area of Pennsylvania that had been under dispute by both the Pennsylvania government and the Connecticut government. The background of this dispute revolved around the need for cheap land and conflicting interpretations of Connecticut's charter with the king, dated 1662. With the state of Connecticut growing rapidly, in 1753, the Susquehanna Company was formed. The company acquired a deed from some Indian chiefs for a large tract of land along the Susquehanna River, about one-third of it in the colony of Pennsylvania. With both Pennsylvania and Connecticut claiming the territory, the Connecticut group took its claim to the crown and received a favorable reply from England in 1773. Pennsylvania did not give up the land and appointed a committee to seek a peaceful settlement, which failed. People from Connecticut sided with the British, believing that the British would uphold their claim to the land. Those from Pennsylvania took the side of the Continental government. Between the years of 1769 and 1794, before, during and after the American Revolution, the Connecticut settlers and their militias fought with the militias of the Pennsylvania colonists in a series of wars known as the Yankee-Pennamite Wars. One such conflict occurred in July 1778.

The Iroquois Confederacy had been conspiring with the British and Tories for months to plan an attack on the Wyoming settlement. Carried out in July 1778, "The plan was arranged that the Mohawk Colonel, Joseph Brant, would create a diversion in the north while Sakayengwaraghton, a

Seneca chief, led his warriors into the Susquehanna Valley. Details were worked out at a conference at Montreal."[113] "The defenders of Forty Fort [refugee settlers] were fighting for their homes and for the survival of a great humanitarian ideal embodied in the new nation to whose cause they committed their lives...not only a three-to-one superiority [by the Indians] in numbers but also the revival among the Indians of old memories coupled with a determination to recover their lost valley."[114] The fort was taken by the Indians. While there have been stories of a massacre of settlers, historians discount these as folklore—although there was violence on outlying farms. The true Massacre of Wyoming happened on the battlefield not among the refugees at Forty Fort.

An Indian-Loyalist force of 500 marched south into the Wyoming Valley. Demanding the surrender of the fort, the commander and his senior officers debated whether to stay in the fort and wait for reinforcements or move out and confront the raiders. Shortly before noon on July 3, 1778, the commanding officer and 386 militiamen marched out of Forty Fort to battle the British-Indian force. By 3:00 p.m., the force arrived at Wintermoot, which was on fire. While the Continental force was calling on the British-Indian force to surrender, the British-Indian force was waiting for them in the woods. Surprising the Continentals, the British-Indian force prevailed. For the rest of the day, the militiamen were tortured, slain and, in some cases, scalped. Approximately 300 were killed, and the Indians took the scalps of 227 Continental soldiers. The Wyoming Valley was largely depopulated of white settlers after the summer of 1778. This episode in American history led to the Sullivan campaign against the Iroquois in Pennsylvania and New York in 1779.

By September 1778, the Americans, in order to encourage the Delaware to join with them, proposed a treaty at Pittsburgh, offering the tribe admission to the Union as a fourteenth Indian state. The Indian chief White Eyes, who had been successful in keeping the Delaware neutral for a few more months after the "Squaw Massacre" and who was pro-American, was involved in the treaty. Sadly, he died. Congress did not act to ratify the treaty. The Delaware joined the British.

19.

General Sullivan's Scorched-Earth Campaign

In 1779, George Washington called on Gershom Hicks to complete a secret spy mission on behalf of the American cause. For Hicks, this was a transformative event that further repaired the reputation that had been cast on him by the British. Absent from his unit on the command of General Washington around March 1 or earlier, Hicks went into Iroquois country and successfully journeyed from "Wyalusing to Niagara and Back," having crossed the southern part of the state of New York.[115]

The mission was filled with danger. According to the accounts of the assignment, Washington had sent other scouts to spy on his behalf, but only Gershom Hicks returned. His years among the Indians were invaluable in this endeavor. Posing as an Indian, he penetrated Indian country, undiscovered, until he arrived in Chemung, New York, where he had no problem talking with the enemy. Chemung is an Indian name meaning "horn" or "antlers."[116]

A letter from Colonel William Patterson to George Washington on April 3, 1779, reads:

> *Hicks met with twenty-five of the troops in pay of Britain and about thirty warriors of the Mingo, Munsey, and Tuscarora Tribes. The whites were commanded by a Serjet, who told Hicks the officer was gone to the lake to meet a reinforcmt* [sic] *of troops, the Serjt said he knew but little more than there was an expedition talked of among the officers and Indians, that the Six Nations and their dependents*

> *were all preparing for war, those at Shamong live on corn, sugar, and wild meat.…He, Hicks, saw sundries, empty pork and fllour* [sic] *barrels and a few prisoners.…From everything Hicks cou'd hear, he thinks Shamong and the other towns nearest will soon be evacuated and their inhabitants take shelter under the bark of the Senekee Country at and near a town call'd the big Ax on the waters of Lake Ontaria, about sixty or seventy miles from Shamong—the distance between the navigable waters of the Alegeny and Cayuga branch for small boats about thirty-five miles, the country leavel* [sic] *but in part Swampey Beetchland.…* [Hicks] *says the enimy* [sic] *treated him rough at first, but, in the end, kind, that the party* [that] *attacked Wyoming were not from Shamong.…That on his return, he tracked warriors at the head of Munsey Creeck* [sic], *steering their course towards Sunbury, on his way up, heard several guns fired near Wyalusing, there is a small Stokade a little below Shamong but no one in it, he further says there are several empty houses in the town appears to have been long evacuated as they used them for cow stables and quantities of dung lie in them.*[117]

As Hicks was traveling down the north branch of the Susquehanna River, from Iroquois Country, later in the month of March, a letter was sent from Colonel William Patterson, who was commanding at Fort Augusta (Sunbury, Pennsylvania), to Colonel Zebulon Butler, who was commanding at Fort Wyoming (Wilkes-Barre, Pennsylvania), and it read as follows:

> *Mr. Lemmon, goe* [sic] *to your post, to wait the return, and take into his care Gershom Hicks, who is not to be examined or searched until he goes before His Excellency Gen. Washington. I inclose* [sic] *you His Excellency's letter. Be careful that your people, who are out on duty, or fatigue, receive Hicks, who may appear painted, and in a canoe. His regimentals* [i.e., uniform] *I have sent to Mr. Lemmon.*[118]

Arrangements were made to send Hicks straight to Washington's headquarters, and a pass was issued for him on March 25, 1779: "This will serve as a passport for Gershom Hicks, who may appear in Indian dress, and the officer commanding will receive him. W. Patterson."[119]

Hicks had been able to penetrate Indian country undiscovered. His most important discovery was that the British had no supplies or ammunition at Chemung and that a small fort nearby was unoccupied. Gershom Hicks received $300 and expenses [most likely Continental currency]. Colonel Patterson also said he placed Mrs. Hicks and their children with his own family in order to have him "under [his] eye ready for the same services." Washington objected to the expenses, as they were large and appeared to have ended Hicks's career in espionage.[120]

There were several other American spies expected to come in from Iroquois country. General Washington gave orders to Colonel Butler at Wyoming:

> *Persons presenting themselves at your post with passports signed by Colonel William Patterson, as to be suffered to pass and repass without interruption, and without search of their canoes or baggage; they are farther to be supplied with five days provision on their applying for it; and you will afford them any other assistance their circumstances may require.*[121]

The same order was sent to other locations, such as Fort Augusta and Fort Willis, but only Hicks returned. I would offer that it was an amazing feat, except for the fact that Gershom Hicks, a White Indian, was skilled at what he did because he had spent those years as a captive. Was he a great villain? In this instance, no. And in this bit of espionage on behalf of the Continental authorities, he displayed great courage and deserves to be remembered for his contribution to the cause of liberty.

In June 1779, Washington ordered Major General John Sullivan and Brigadier General James Clinton to conduct a campaign against the Iroquois Confederacy in the area where Hicks had conducted his espionage. The aim of the campaign was to break the morale of the confederacy as Sullivan's troops destroyed more than forty Iroquois villages and stores of winter crops, breaking the power of the Six Nations in New York, all the way to the Great Lakes. As revenge for the Wyoming Valley Massacre, Sullivan carried out a scorched-earth campaign. George Washington became known among the Indians as "Town Destroyer." The campaign left the Iroquois totally dependent on the British during the harsh winter of 1779. Many of the Indian survivors fled to Canada.

This area of western Pennsylvania (the Pennsylvania Wilds) was not immune from the settlers' push into Indian lands. One such action in 1779 was conducted by Colonel Brodhead, who was under the command of General Sullivan (the same General Sullivan who carried out the scorched-earth policy in New York State). Launching a raid at

Thompson's Island, nine miles below Conewango, near present-day Warren, Broadhead's troops torched the Seneca Cornplanter's town, destroying five hundred acres of corn, and they left quickly before the Indians could retaliate.

Part IV

A NEW NATION

20.
Exploring the Pennsylvania Wilds

The Treaty of Paris was finally signed on September 3, 1783, with the British recognizing the independence of its former colonies as the United States of America, with boundaries extending west to the Mississippi; north to Canada, with fishing rights in Newfoundland; and south to Florida. While the treaty addressed British rights to the colonies, it did not address Indian rights to land.

Following the Revolutionary War, the United States made peace with the Natives in a series of treaties. One early treaty, signed following the French and Indian War, was the Fort Stanwix Treaty of 1768, which set up a line following the Ohio River that was a permanent boundary between the Indians and white settlers. The Natives hoped it would end the push by white settlers into their lands—but that was not to be. Settlers, land speculators and the newly formed United States government eventually wanted to extinguish Native land rights beyond the Ohio Valley, and another treaty was made at Fort Stanwix with the Six Nations (Iroquois Confederacy) in 1784. While the treaty was ratified by the United States in 1785, it was never ratified by the Natives. By 1795, a compromise was made following the Battle of Fallen Timber the year before. Increasingly, the white settlers pushed into Native lands.

***

The section of Pennsylvania that has been designated the Pennsylvania Wilds is composed of Warren, McKean, Potter, Tioga, Lycoming, Clinton,

Elk, Cameron, Forest, Clearfield, Clarion and Jefferson Counties and the northern portion of Centre Counties. These counties encompass a small section of the state that was known as the Last Purchase of 1784, the surrender of Native lands in western Pennsylvania and Ohio. In Pennsylvania, that land area was made up of twenty-three counties—namely, Allegheny, Armstrong, Beaver, Bradford, Butler, Cameron, Clarion, Clearfield, Clinton, Crawford, Elk, Erie, Forest, Indiana, Jefferson, Lawrence, Lycoming, McKean, Mercer, Potter, Tioga, Venango and Warren.

On April 9, 1790, at the direction of the Supreme Executive Council of Pennsylvania, Samuel Maclay, Timothy Matlack and John Adlum made an expedition into the West Branch of the Susquehanna, Sinnemahoning and Allegheny Rivers, hoping to find a possible route for a road to connect the waters of the Allegheny River with the West Branch of the Susquehanna River. The journey lasted five months. Guiding the men were Thomas Semor, Gershom Hicks and Matthew Gray. This journey was a trek into what was then certainly the Pennsylvania Wilds, as not many settlers had yet established homesteads in the region.

Clarion River Below Portland Mills, Elk County. Courtesy of Andrew Myers.

Clarion River Below Hallton and Above Belltown, Elk County. Courtesy of Andrew Myers.

The Journal of Samuel Maclay was published by John P. Megenness in 1887, some ninety-seven years after the journey. It is an interesting account of the day-to-day struggle to push through the wilderness and achieve their goal of penetrating the newly purchased lands in northwestern Pennsylvania. The guides, Semor, Hicks and Gray, had various duties from taking care of packhorses and canoes, to finding game for meals, cooking meals over campfires and walking for miles through the wilderness in all kinds of weather as they guided the three men who were appointed to make the expedition. On one June morning, Maclay ordered Hicks to put some chocolate on to boil for breakfast, an interesting choice for rugged men in the wilderness.

Through its chapters, I found the names of the locations in today's Pennsylvania Wilds that have been familiar to me since my childhood. There is a notation about the Great Elk Lick, which is some ten miles north of Emporium near Sizerville. It was said that "ground around for at least 3 acres was virtually cleared of brush by the stamping herds of elk and deer [in their quest to lick the salt]."[122] The notation also reported that the area of "Potter, McKean and Elk Counties, and what is now Cameron County, was the last retreat for the elk." By 1841, there was a known herd of thirteen, which were slain one by one until they were extinct.[123]

There is mention of the Big Elk Lick located at Trout Run, near Benezette. Today, Benezette is home to the Elk Country Visitor Center, where the Pennsylvania Game Commission has succeeded in establishing the only elk herd east of the Mississippi River in this area of the Pennsylvania Wilds, where they formerly roamed freely when Maclay and company passed through here. Not far from Benezette is the place known as Hicks Run on the Bennett's Branch of the Sinnemahoning Creek, named for Gershom Hicks.

The five-month adventure took them through what was to become Ridgway, my hometown and now the county seat of Elk County, along the waterway that was known as the Toby, now referred to as the Clarion River. Here and there along the way, the party met some interesting characters, including a Dutchman who had been taken captive by the Indians and who chose to stay with them, as well as the notable David Mead, the founder of Meadville, a major general and, eventually, an associate judge in Crawford County. Mead was also a charter member of Allegheny College.

By July, the party was near what is today Warren, Pennsylvania. On July 7, Maclay reported his meeting with Cornplanter, king of the Seneca and son of a trader by the name of O'Bail (O'Ball) and a Seneca woman. A contemporary of George Washington, Cornplanter had a long history of war with the colonials. He was involved in the defeat of General Braddock at Fort Duquesne in 1754. However, later in his life, he signed on to the Treaties of Fort Stanwix and Fort Harmar. Once Cornplanter was won over from the French, he maintained his allegiance to the new government during the Indian Wars (1790–1794).[124]

On learning of the plans to locate a road to connect the Allegheny River with the Susquehanna River, Cornplanter and his people were glad to have received that information, as "they would be able to purchase what things they wanted on better terms."[125]

> *In 1789, the Society for Promoting the Improvement of Road and Inland navigation was formed. Surveys of the Schuylkill, Susquehanna, and other streams were authorized with a view of ascertaining the cost of the proposed waterways to connect with the lakes to bring trade to Philadelphia. In 1791,* [following Maclay's journey] *the society…submitted a report to the legislature, giving a comprehensive view of the various routes for canals and roads.*[126]

Maclay kept a detailed record of the routes and costs associated with those various routes. The following is the record of the miles presented in his report:

> *Susquehanna navigation as connected with the Schuylkill on the east and Ohio and the Great Lakes on the west: from Philadelphia to Pittsburgh, 425 miles;*
>
> *From Philadelphia to Presque Isle by the West Branch of the Susquehanna, Sinnemahoning and Conewango, 524 miles;*
>
> *Another route to the lakes is also given as follows:*
>
> *From Philadelphia to the Forks of the Sinnemahoning, 326 miles*
> *Up the West Branch of the Sinnemahoning, 24 miles*
> *Portage to Little Toby Creek to the main branch, 10 miles*
> *Down the main branch of Little Toby Creek to Allegheny, 70 miles*
> *Up the Allegheny to French Creek, 35 miles*
> *Up French Creek and the Portage to Presque Isle, 31 miles*
>
> *For a total of 560 miles*[127]

Within my home region, I can visualize this last route at the forks of the Sinnemahoning Creek, with its various twists and turns. Eventually, the expedition explored French Creek and the Portage to Presque Isle, the very location where Gershom Hicks had picked grapes for the Indians all those years ago, an experience he related to John Adlum, another member of the expedition.

21. Witness Trees

"I think that I shall never see a poem lovely as a tree," words penned by Joyce Kilmer describing the beauty of the species. As a child born in autumn in the Pennsylvania Wilds, I believed that the changing color of the leaves was in honor of my birthday. The bright reds and warm golds of those bygone days are forever burned into my memory. As an adult, I came to realize the importance of trees in the early history of our region. Trees of many species provided shade, fruit and nuts for humans and animals alike, home-building materials, fuel to warm the homes of the settlers and, later, the pulp to manufacture paper. Trees were spiritual, playing a role in tombstone art. The weeping willow, as one example, is the symbol of perpetual mourning or grief. We speak of family trees in genealogy, and the Bible speaks of the Tree of Life. Trees had another more practical purpose in Colonial times. Trees were used to mark property lines.

I had never given much thought to how the colony of Pennsylvania went about divvying up the vast acres of land that became the Commonwealth of Pennsylvania until I was having a conversation a few years ago with my son, a registered professional archaeologist. He was discussing a survey he was conducting and used the term witness tree. I had never heard that term before and became fascinated with the subject. He explained that witness trees are trees that date back to colonial times, when surveyors would mark trees located on the corner of large parcels of land, known as warrants, that were to be registered with the proprietary government for sale.

Marked line tree, surveyor's tree of choice, maple. *Courtesy of John Myers.*

William Penn established a Proprietary Land Office in 1682, which detailed the sectioning off of vast tracts of land. The Proprietary Land Office went through a series of changes over the years. "After the outbreak of the Revolutionary War, the Proprietary Land Office ceased to function. The Divesting Act of 1779 transferred ownership of most of the remaining 22 million acres of proprietary lands to the Commonwealth....By 1843, this process was turned over to the surveyor general."[128] According to the Land Office, "Land records are among the best-preserved public documents. While some of the records have disappeared through neglect, or vanished into private collections, the great majority of Pennsylvania's land records were well preserved, and most of even the earliest records are still available for public inspection."[129] The methods adopted by Penn continue today.

The methodology of locating archaeological sites by identifying witness trees is simple. Before the archaeologists go into the field to locate Native American or early colonial sites, they refer to the historic warrant maps to assist in locating the survey area. In some instances, the existence of surviving witness trees confirms the site location.

A recent study of witness trees at previously identified archaeological sites in Warren County was conducted by forestry professionals from the Forest Resources Laboratory at Penn State University. The study was to determine forest composition in the upper Allegheny River in 1779 and involved sites occupied by the Seneca, which were destroyed under the direction of Colonel Broadhead, as noted in an earlier chapter. "Forest conditions were characterized by tallying witness trees from original warrant maps (1790–1820) that represent a tract of land as surveyed at the time of European settlement (Munger 1991)....European settlement of the Allegheny River area began after the purchase of northwestern Pennsylvania in 1789."[130]

Much was expected of the early surveyors.

> *The role of the surveyor in the early growth of this nation is of utmost importance. The boundaries of the vast land grants had to be determined, and the constant disputes of the grantees had to be fairly adjudicated.*

> *The lands on which towns and cities would be built had to be surveyed, cleared, and devised into small lots. The lands of the farmer had to be surveyed, marked out, and recorded. Not only was the surveyor responsible for these tasks, but the citizens also depended on him for reporting settler and Indian movements, maintaining contact between the cities and the outlying settlements, evaluating available land for habitation and speculation, serving as a representative of the lands' proprietors and aiding them in completing the many legal forms that were necessary.*[131]

In those early years, two of the favorite tree species chosen by surveyors to become witness trees were the then-plentiful chestnut and white oak. Selecting trees with a "grub" (or deformity) made them less likely to be taken down by lumbermen; the trees were blazed, a method of cutting into the living tissue deep enough to make a mark that would last for many years.[132] While existing witness trees are rare, other marked trees that exist in the region represent long-ago agreed-on property lines that were marked in a similar fashion.

The history of land transactions in this region can be traced to the Holland Land Company.

> *The Holland Land Company was an unincorporated syndicate of thirteen Dutch investors from Amsterdam who purchased the western two-thirds of the Phelps and Gorham Purchase, an area that, afterward, was known as the Holland Purchase. Aliens were forbidden from owning land within the United States, so the investors placed their funds in the hands of certain trustees, who bought the land in central and western New York State and western Pennsylvania. The syndicate hoped to sell the land rapidly at a great*

Marked corner tree, the surveyor's tree of choice, beech. *Courtesy of John Myers.*

Marked corner trees, the surveyor's tree of choice, beech. *Courtesy John of Myers.*

profit. Instead, for many years, they were forced to make further investments in their purchase; surveying it, building roads, digging canals, to make it more attractive to settlers. They sold the last of their land interests in 1840, when the syndicate was dissolved.[133]

A familiar name on many warrant maps in this region is Wilhelm Willink.

75,000 Acres of Land Will be sold at Public Sale, to the Highest Bidder, on Saturday, the first day of April next, at 12 o'clock at the Merchants' Coffeehouse, in the city of Philadelphia.

The Holland Land Company, desirous to promote the settlement and population of the interior parts of the state and open the sale of their lands in the 6 east Allegany districts, offer 75 tracts of land containing about 990 acres each, at public sale.

These lands are situated in the 3d or Canan's District, and in the Counties of McKean and Clearfield, near the navigable waters of the Susquehanna. The soil is good and well-watered by several streams, viz the Sinnemahoning and Kockeketow Creeks and Bennet's Branch (some of them boatable) fall into the West Branch of the Susquehanna.

A good Wagon Road has been opened from the mouth of the Baldeagle Creek, on the West Branch of the Susquehanna, up the navigable waters of the Sinnemahoning to the Driftwood, and thence continued, in a northwesterly direction, to the state line; where it intersects another road,

> *which crossing the Allegany River, passes through the Genesee Territory, to the outlet of the Cattaraugus River, into Lake Erie, opening the shortest route to Upper Canada.*[134]

Another advertisement appeared in 1813, offering land in Jefferson County:

> *118 Tracts of lands in Jefferson county, containing about 990 acres and allowance in each tract, situated on the waters of Toby's Creek, Spring Creek, Beaver-Dam, Towanista and Trout Creek. These lands will be sold either by wholesale or single tracts, to suit the purchasers.*[135]

With the earliest deed in a chain of title to my property in Jefferson County, part of Warrant #2975, recorded in the Jefferson County Courthouse in 1846, the recital for prior deeds lists the Holland Land Company as the grantor in a time while Jefferson County was still under the jurisdiction of Indiana County. W. Willink & Co. (Willink had been part of the Holland Land Company) acquired the 900.75 acres that became Warrant #2975 on December 13, 1792. Along the southern boundary line of my 41.00-acre property, trees that were marked by early surveyors still stand. While the markings on my property are not as old as the witness trees that mark the original corners of the warrant, they are testimonies to a recognized line made in an earlier time by the original settlers.

The forest composition of northwest Pennsylvania has changed over the years. Due to intense timbering, gone are the big stands of the ancient hemlock and white pine. Some species of trees simply died off, an example being the chestnut that did not survive the chestnut blight. Today, this region of Pennsylvania is a mixed hardwoods region, with Kane, Pennsylvania, in McKean County, being known as the black cherry capital of the world.[136]

The forests were so thick in the early years of railroading (1864) that

> *early passengers boarding trains at Warren would have noted that when they crossed the Allegheny River, they entered what appeared to be a swath cut through the woods, much as though a reaper had gone through and mowed with a scythe. Their impression of it would be much the same as a traveler passing through a long tunnel today. The timber was so dense, the sunlight seldom penetrated to the forest floor, and engine crews had to light the lamps in the cab to read the steam gauge.... The hemlock grew in immense stands so thick they shut out the sunlight, and the trees were large.*

> *Many stumps easily measured four feet or more in diameter….A tree cut near Nansen in Highland Township, Elk County, measured eight feet across the stump.*[137]

While the old growth forests are, for the most part, gone and coming across witness trees is rare, trees remain important to the economy of the Wilds. Both the timber industry and various forms of outdoor recreation, including camping, hiking, hunting, cross-country skiing, biking, trekking and snowmobile riding, are alive and well in the Wilds.

22.

1816

The Year Without a Summer

The "year without a summer" was an oddity of nature that caused frosts in widespread locations throughout the states. Hardest hit were the New England states; however, New York and areas of Pennsylvania also suffered from the unusually cold weather.

In an article carried in the *United States Gazette* (Philadelphia), a description was given of the weather from the *Brattleborough Reporter* (Vermont) on July 17, 1816:

> *The Season—it is believed that the memory of no man living can furnish a parallel to the present season. From every part of the United States north from the Potomack* [sic], *as well as from Canada, we have accounts of the remarkable coldness of the weather, and of vegetation discarded or destroyed by the untimely frosts."*[138]

Another article, appearing in a newspaper sixty-two years after the occurrence, carried the following remembrance: "The summerless year, old farmers refer to it as 'eighteen hundred and starve to death.'"[139]

This freak of nature was responsible for people in the areas most affected to depend on hunters from areas such as western Pennsylvania to supply them with meat and fish. In other words, it provided the region's early settlers with a new opportunity for revenue.

But the freak of nature had other outcomes—the migrations of people from the areas most affected into the areas less affected including the Wilds region. There are records of several families arriving in Elk, Clearfield and Jefferson Counties from New England and New York State in 1818, two years after the disastrous year without a summer. It is possible they came for the promise of cheap land offered by the Holland Land Company, but the weather may have had a definite impact on their relocation, as history records the year of 1816 as a time of migration for many groups of people. One of the better-known group of migrants was the Joseph Smith family from Vermont, who moved to New York State and brought on a series of events that led to the founding of the Mormon Church.[140]

The event wasn't really understood until one hundred years after the occurrence. Evidence has proven that the year without a summer was caused by volcanic activity in 1815 at Mount Tambour in the Dutch East Indies, known today as Indonesia.[141] Areas across the globe were affected. From Brookville, a local historian, William McKnight, wrote the following:

> *1816, or the year without a summer. Frost occurred in every month in 1816. Ice formed half an inch thick in May. Snow fell to the depth of three inches in June. Ice was formed to the thickness of a common window-glass on the 5th day of July. Indian corn was so frozed* [sic] *that the greater part was cut in August and dried for fodder, and the pioneers supplied from the corn of 1815 for the seeding of the spring of 1817.*[142]

Part V

Collection of Stories From the Wilds

23.
Cameron County

Cameron County is a wild and wonderful outdoor paradise. Visitors looking to unplug from their busy lives are attracted to the area to connect with nature and unwind in the quiet mountains.
—Pennsylvania Great Outdoors Visitors Bureau[143]

Cameron County was created on March 29, 1860, from parts of Clinton, McKean, Elk, and Potter Counties. Named for U.S. senator Simon Cameron, it is one of the more recent counties to be established in the Pennsylvania Wilds. Comprising 381 square miles, or 243,840 acres of land, in the 2010 census, Cameron County had 5,085 inhabitants, making it the least-populated county in the Commonwealth of Pennsylvania.

Sinnemahoning Creek and its tributaries played an important role in the settlement of the county. The main tributary for the West Branch of the Susquehanna River, its name is derived from a corruption of an Indian name, Achsini-mahoni, or "stony lick."[144] Early settlers who were coming into the county followed Indian paths that had been chiefly used by the Seneca.

> *An Indian trail ran up the West Branch, from Shamokin (Sunbury) to the Big Island (Lock Haven), and then on up the West Branch, along the northern shore to the Sinnemahoning to Emporium, and then over the divide to the Allegheny, which it reached at the present Port Allegany, McKean County….There were several branches of this trail at various points, leading northward into the Genesee Valley.*[145]

Left: Cameron County Courthouse in Emporium, Pennsylvania. *Courtesy of Wikimedia Commons.*

Below: Sinnemahoning Creek. *Courtesy of Nicholas A., www.Tonelli@flicker.com.*

When Samuel Maclay, Timothy Matlack and John Adlum made their expedition into the West Branch of the Susquehanna, Sinnemahoning and Allegheny Rivers, which was referenced in an earlier chapter, they described their time surveying the Sinnemahoning Creek area near a spot known as First Fork, now the Village of Sinnemahoning. On June 16, 1790, it was noted, "There were no white settlers in this section. It was a very wild place—in fact, a 'howling wilderness.'"[146]

If a person is looking for archaeological evidence for Native Americans, Cameron County, which remains a remote area, is underrepresented in Pennsylvania Archaeological Site Survey files. There is some evidence that the Susquehanna or Conestoga Indians had hunting camps at the mouth of Sterling Run, which "is still the wildest and most sparsely settled [area] in the entire state."[147]

There was, however, one interesting find recorded in one of the histories of the county. It was said that, in 1873, the post office building at Sterling Run was moved about forty feet from its location, which necessitated the digging of a cellar. The man in charge, a Mr. Earl, while inspecting the site, found human bones, which on closer examination, turned out to be seventeen skeletons, which he believed to be of Native origin. The report notes that all but two were of ordinary stature. One measured seven and a half feet from the top of its skull to the heel; there was also a smaller body. The skeletons appeared to have been relaxing, possibly some sleeping, as they were arranged in a three-quarter circle with their feet to the fire (residue ashes and coals were found). Some had their heads to the east, some to the north and others to the west. One skeleton had a clay pipe between its teeth and a vase by its side made of earthenware or stoneware. The vase was filled with what appeared to be chopped tobacco stems or seeds.

The theory of the day was that the Natives were relaxing or sleeping in a hut by a fire when an electrical storm suddenly developed, and they were struck with lightening. Debris from the hut fell on the bodies where they remained, possibly for centuries, under the rubble where they were found.[148]

A Boy of Ten

On a peaceful early morning in May 1778, young children had gathered in their family's cabin for breakfast with their father and mother, Levi Hicks (a White Indian discussed in an earlier chapter) and Mrs. Hicks (an Indian or half-Indian woman). Levi and his wife were involved in running a mill at Spruce Creek in Huntingdon County, having been there for about three years. Spruce Creek is located along the Penn's Creek Path known among the Iroquois as the Karondinhah Path, which was commonly described on eighteenth-century surveys as a "warriors' path."[149]

That May morning occurred during the time known as the "Great Runaway." With rumors of Indian raids in the area, the Hicks family was urged to seek refuge in either Lytle's Fort or Lowry's Fort. But Hicks felt confident that he was safe, as he had lived among the Indians for so many years after being taken prisoner at the Great Cove Massacre in 1755. So, on this particular morning, as was his custom, Levi started the mill and joined his family in the cabin for breakfast. Following his morning repast, he returned to the mill, sitting in the doorway as he repaired his moccasins. His wife soon joined him there.

Hearing a rustling in the woods surrounding the mill, Hicks made the mistake of walking out in a casual way rather than being on alert. It cost him his life. He was shot through the heart by an Indian. His wife, hearing the shot, ran to the creek and crossed over to the other side, making her way to Lytle's Fort for help. On her way, she came across a horseman, who rode ahead of her with the alarm. It was then that she turned and saw her ten-year-old son, very possibly Levi Hicks Jr., following behind her. The other children had been left in the cabin.

They had no help until the next day, when men from the fort found Hicks dead and scalped. His young daughter, who had apparently left the cabin when she heard the shot, was found scalped but alive, having crawled back into the cabin. While she lived on for a few years, she was never right again. The other children were safe, one being a baby in a cradle.

Levi Hicks was buried on the property, and the mill was shuttered for several years. There was no information provided about the tribe that attacked the Hicks family.[150] Levi Hicks Jr., who was present at the attack, became one of the early settlers of Cameron County, arriving with Andrew Overturf and Samuel Smith in 1806. He settled between First Fork and Second Fork, where he cleared about thirty acres of land. By 1812, Hicks moved to the mouth of Hicks Run. It is said that Hicks Run was named for his uncle White Indian Gershom Hicks. Levi Hicks Jr., who was approximately thirty-five years old when he came to the region, is known for running the first raft down the Sinnemahoning River.[151] What skills did he learn from his Indian-captive father, skills that he carried with him into Cameron County?

While history does not reveal the purpose of Hicks's rafting trip, timbering became an early industry in the region. To meet demands in the larger cities, the early settlers, during periods of nonagricultural work, took up the slack with the sale of lumber. Cameron County became one of those areas in which "farmer-raftsmen" harvested valuable white pines, among other species.[152]

Revenge

In 1778, the year known as the "Great Runaway," a man named James Brady, a relative of one Peter Grove, was killed on August 8 by an Indian attack on a group of soldiers on the Loyal Sock in Lycoming County. Following this incident, two men named Grove and their friend were determined to take revenge on the Indians. Locating their trail, they followed the Indians to the mouth of the Tangascootack Creek (Scootack Creek), a tributary of the

Susquehanna River in Clinton County, and then up the valley to the mouth of Sinnemahoning Creek (corruption of Achsini-mahoni, or "stony lick").[153]

The men found the Indians camped near the mouth of what has since been named Grove's Run, near the town of Sinnemahoning. Just below the run, twelve Indians stuck their hatchets in a large oak and made a small fire before lying down to sleep. Another Indian remained awake, sitting against the tree with the hatchets, acting as sentry while the others slept. While Peter Grove and the others waited nearby for an opportune moment to attack, eventually the sentry nodded off. Grove and his companions killed the sentry and seven other Indians; one Indian fled with a hatchet in his back, and four escaped. The men broke the locks on the Indian guns and threw them into the creek. They made their way to the river, climbed a mountain and could see twenty-five warriors on their trail. After a brief rest, the three made their way to a settlers' fort. While they were still seven miles from the fort, they again saw the twenty-five Indians on their trail. The Indians lost the trail of the three men as they made their way into the river.

According to the old history, a white oak at today's Grove Run, the same tree where the Indians had stuck their tomahawks, "was about thirty inches in diameter; a smooth, handsome body, but short, being about twenty feet to the lowest limb. It stood there, with the marks of the thirteen hatchets until after the great flood of October 8, 1847, the waters of which washed the clay from its roots, leaving it to decay and to the mercy of the great flood of 1861, which carried it away. About the year 1820, the pond at the mouth of Grove Creek, where the battle occurred, was drained and a gun barrel and lock found, which had not been recovered by the Indians. The marks of a dozen tomahawks were visible in the limb of the old oak tree until it fell into the river."[154]

Captured

When Samuel Smith arrived in Cameron County with Levi Hicks and Andrew Overturf in 1806, he was a single man, approximately twenty-one years of age. He was the son of Jacob Smith and the grandson of an amazing Revolutionary War Patriot, the widow Catherine Smith. Widow Smith, with her ten children, settled at the mouth of White Deer Creek in Union County around 1773 on three hundred acres of land that had been claimed by her late husband, Peter Smith. Catherine and her sons built a gristmill to process grain and a sawmill to cut local lumber. Later, a boring mill was added. Boring mills made rifle barrels and rebored barrels as they became worn from use, and her mill served the Revolutionary militia.

During the "Great Runaway," which occurred in 1778, Widow Smith's mills were burned down by the Indians, and she was forced to seek refuge elsewhere. Returning to White Deer to rebuild the flour and sawmills in 1793, she was ejected from the land. No deed had ever been filed by her husband to prove ownership, and the property was claimed by two men from Philadelphia, Claypole and Morris. Catherine Smith petitioned the Pennsylvania Assembly for the return of the property and payment for her work for the Revolutionary militia. She walked to Philadelphia, 160 miles each way, several times to have her case heard. She was unsuccessful in restoring the land in her name, and others took over the mills. The government never paid her for her work.[155] Today, a historical marker, *Catherine's Crown* stands in her honor in White Deer Township. Samuel Smith came from hardy pioneer stock.

In the 1820 census, Samuel Smith and his family were residing in Gibson Township, Clearfield County (now Cameron County). There were nine people in the household, including five males under the age of ten; two males aged twenty-six to forty-four; one male aged forty-five and over; and one female aged sixteen to twenty-five. This reveals that Samuel and his wife had five sons at that time, and there were two older males who were also living with them, possibly in-laws or hired hands. It was a large household to be cared for.

Samuel Smith has gone down in the history of Cameron County not for his grandmother's patriotism during the Revolution or for the number of children he fathered, but rather, for two fugitives who were captured at his home. In the latter part of June 1820, when law enforcement was sparse to nonexistent in that region of Pennsylvania, the sheriff of Centre County arrived with a posse of twelve armed men who were pursuing two robbers, Connelly and Lewis, who were to be captured either dead or alive. Connelly and Lewis were well-known "highwaymen." Some in the population compared them to Dick Turpin, a famous "highwayman" from Hempstead, England, who was a robber and a horse thief whose exploits were romanticized as a sort of Robin Hood character—in other words, it was said that Connelly and Lewis robbed from the rich and gave to the poor. Their most-recent escapade was to commit a robbery at General Potter's Store in Penn's Valley, Centre County. To escape the long arm of the law, the robbers made their way to the wilderness of the

Sinnemahoning Branch, where Lewis's mother and brother lived. The posse was formed to bring them to justice.

With the trail leading into what was then Clearfield County (now Cameron County), there were no established roads, and travel was slow. After following the Driftwood branch of the Sinnemahoning Creek for eighteen miles through the underbrush, no tracks were found. The group of men turned to follow the second branch to Grove Creek. At Grove Creek, they met a man named David Brooks, who had just come from his father's home in Driftwood. After a discussion with the posse, Brooks told them that two strangers were seen going up the Driftwood branch. Brooks agreed to join the posse as a guide. Along the way, at Tanglefoot Run, approximately half a mile below the residence of Samuel Smith, they met William Shephard, who lived at the mouth of the Bennett's Branch. Shepherd happened to be on his way home from Smith's house, where he had been at a party that morning, firing at targets and indulging in "old rye." The posse, in questioning Shepherd, learned that the two robbers were there, shooting mark and mingling with the crowd. They persuaded Shepherd to return to the Smith property, and they asked him to privately inform Smith and his family that they were in danger. Meanwhile, Brooks took the posse on a path through the woods, to a hill overlooking Smith's residence, which was about one hundred feet away.

There are two versions of the story of what occurred at Samuel Smith's home. One says that, as Shepherd arrived at the house, someone called out "treat," and his message for Smith was delayed while he took a drink. The other version is that Shepherd vowed the posse would not take the men. Is it possible that he believed the robbers did rob from the rich to give to the poor? Whether Shepherd's actions were affected by the "treat" he drank or he didn't want them captured, Shepherd failed to warn Smith privately that the posse was in the bushes at the top of the hill; instead, he yelled out, "Take care of yourselves, the sheriff and his men are here." The posse charged over the hill, firing their guns as they ran. Connelly grabbed his gun when the alarm was given. Lewis was shot in the arm and surrendered. Connelly was shot in the abdomen but ran across the field, toward the river, leaping over fences. On reaching a potato field, he turned, aiming his gun toward his pursuers; however, it was unloaded, and he had dropped his ammunition. Connelly fled into the bushes and was lost from sight. The posse arrived at the home of Benjamin Brooks, an old Revolutionary soldier (who was probably the father of David Brooks), who met them in his front yard, demanding an explanation. As the posse was explaining their mission to Mr.

Brooks, believing that the robber had escaped up the mountain, one of the men caught a glimpse of a piece of clothing. Searching further, they found Connelly lying in the bushes, faint from the loss of blood. Samuel Smith and his family were unharmed.

The two fugitives were then loaded in a canoe and started down the river, pulling into shore while the posse guarded them overnight. The next day, the party arrived at the site where Lock Haven now stands, and from there, they were taken by wagon to the Bellefonte Jail. Connelly died on July 3, 1820. Lewis, whose wounded arm became infected, refused to have it amputated, and he died from gangrene later that July.[156]

The story of the capture was widely covered in several newspapers of the day, including the *Lancaster Intelligencer*, the *Gettysburg Compiler*, the *Wyoming Herald* (Wilkes-Barre) and the *York Gazette*.

24.
Clearfield County

Backwoods, Backroads, Backwaters. Halfway to Everywhere, but Always in Your Heart.[157]

Clearfield County was formed from parts of Lycoming and Huntingdon Counties by an act of assembly that was passed by the legislature on March 20, 1804, and signed by the governor. The county takes its name from the cleared fields that were found, apparently the old cornfields of its earlier inhabitants, the Indians. When the early settlers arrived, the county was almost entirely continuous forest and rugged mountains, making travel difficult. The summit between the borough of Clearfield and the village of Penfield has been recorded as 2,200 feet above sea level.[158]

The natural wonder of Clearfield County can be found in Bilger's Rocks, which, according to the website www.visitclearfieldcounty.org, "is a 300-million-year-old rock formation."

> *Upon entering the many acres of massive rocks, one often feels an eerie sense of being transported through time and space to another era and a different place. You meet with what appears to be a hidden world of mazes, paths and caves leading in all directions, beckoning and inviting you to stay and explore. You find yourself captured and pulled forward by the possibilities and mystery of this unique setting. Shielded in this fantastic vivid landscape by walls of huge megalithic stones, extraordinary hanging vegetation and bizarrely shaped byways, one's imagination is drawn to an*

Left: Clearfield County Courthouse in Clearfield, Pennsylvania. *Courtesy of Wikimedia Commons.*

Below: The highest point on I-80, between the village of Penfield and the borough of Clearfield. *Courtesy of Wikimedia Commons.*

Left: Saint Severin's Old Log Church in Drifting, Pennsylvania, which was built by German Catholic settlers, is listed in the National Register of Historic Places. *Courtesy of Wikimedia Commons.*

Below: Bloody Knox, an example of an early log home. *Courtesy of www.visitclearfieldcounty.org.*

exciting adventure of discovery....Light, shade and temperature take on new meanings as you move through this unusual, ancient geological environment.

Two fine examples of a bygone era in Clearfield County are preserved in buildings that were created from logs. In Drifting stands St. Severin Church, which was built in 1851 and is listed in the Natural Register of Historic Places. Another, an 1860s cabin in Olanta, became famous for a Civil War event that is now known as Bloody Knox.

Clearfield was chosen as the county seat on May 20, 1805, and the first courthouse was built in 1814. The present-day main courthouse was completed in 1862 on the site of the former building, with an addition constructed in 1882. Today, a modern annex has been added to the historic building; it houses several offices, including those for assessment, the district attorney, a judge's chamber and others.

James Woodside

James Woodside is something of an enigma in the history of Clearfield County. Accounts differ as to his date of birth, but it is said that he was thirty-six years old when he arrived in the region, which places his birth in 1749. He was of Irish descent and came from Chester County to this region in 1785 as a chain carrier with a company of surveyors. He returned after being granted Warrant #570 on July 30, 1785, which was surveyed to him. While some credit him with being the first white settler in the region, others disagree. Before the county was established in 1804, the West Branch of the Susquehanna River was a dividing line between those counties that were already established; every settler on the north or west side of the river was located in Lycoming County, while those on the south and east of the River were located in Huntingdon County. Woodside's land was located north and west of the river in what became Brady Township, which was named for Captain Samuel Brady, the famed Indian fighter and hunter. Thus, Woodside was a citizen of Lycoming County at that time. Those who knew him stated that no one visited him for twenty-two years aside from the Indians.[159]

A review of the history of Chester County reveals that Woodside was the son of Archibald Woodside, who was born in Londonderry, Ireland, around 1720, arriving in this country around 1728. His mother was Rachael Stewart, who was born in Northern Ireland. His mother and father were the parents of ten children, with nine surviving to adulthood. The Chester County records reveal that James Woodside and his brother David Woodside, both single men, relocated to Clearfield County. Of his family members, four others were unmarried and remained at the homestead. It seems the family had an aversion to marriage.[160]

James Woodside served in the Revolution and may have received land for his service. The land tax records for Chester County in 1787 list him as "gone"; in 1788, he was listed as a "runaway." In other words, he was not present in Chester County to pay his taxes.[161]

As a child during the unsettling years of the French and Indian War, which raged in Pennsylvania from 1754 to 1764, it is fair to assume that Woodside was exposed to the turmoil of the times. Add to that his service in the Continental army, and it isn't difficult to imagine that on entering the region, he welcomed the peacefulness the vast wilderness afforded him and decided to make this area his home.

A brief description of Woodside reveals that he was "five feet, eight inches high, rather sparely built, weighed about one hundred and forty pounds, had dark brown hair, with florid complexion, all of which betoken that he was of the 'vital-mental' temperament, which indicates brilliancy of intellect and sound health....He possessed a fair education for the times, he was rather reserved in conversation, but always cogent and to the point."[162]

Over the years, other settlers moved into the region and became neighbors of the man who lived alone for twenty-two years. Woodside died in his log cabin at the age of eighty-five in 1834. Fifty years later, in 1885, a celebration was made of Woodside's arrival, which had taken place one hundred years earlier in the Village of Luthersburg, where citizens gathered to remember him. One participant recalled Woodside's time as a hunter and trapper with his long gun and always accompanied by his loyal dog. A man named P.S. Weber read a poem that was written for the *DuBois Courier* by an author who was described as a rising and promising young man. The stanzas of that poem, which present a romanticized version of events, shed further light on this early settler's life:

One hundred years ago to-day
A brave and daring pioneer,
Amid these hills had found his way,
With beating heart that knew no fear.

The wild birds sang among the trees,
The brooks were hid by ferns and moss;
The leaves waved in the gentle breeze,
And fiercer winds their boughs would toss.

The growling wolf and hungry bear,
Crossed o'er his dark and lonely way;
The dismal wood seemed as to dare
The hunter in the gloom to stay.

He traveled on, o'er rock and dale
Until a wigwam in a glen
He found, and there he told his tale
To all the wild and dusky men.

He told of dangers he had met
The cold and hunger he had borne;
They welcomed him, and for him sat
An earthen pot of Indian corn.

They promised peace with him to keep.
As long as he would 'mongst them dwell,
To fish, to hunt, and with him sleep,
And 'round the camp-fires stories tell.

For two and twenty years he stayed
Among the children of the wood,
Ere other white men here had strayed,
And on this lonely ground had stood.

The Indian's gone with bow and spear,
And white men here have come to stay
Since came the hardy pioneer,
One hundred years ago to-day![163]

DANIEL OGDEN

Traveling along the banks of the West Branch of the Susquehanna in Clearfield, I've often reflected on this passageway, which early settlers used to enter this region. The current of the water in the rainy season is swift.

Daniel Ogden, the first man with a family to settle in Clearfield County, arrived in 1797 with three sons in canoes. Their trip was difficult, and at times, passage along the river was narrow and filled with rocks and downed trees. It was not unusual that, in order to pass, the men were forced to unload their canoes, drag them over the obstacles and reload them into the river.

Prior to settling in the Wilds, Ogden was a resident of Cherry Valley, New York, and was a second lieutenant in the Fifth Regiment, New York

State Militia. During the Revolution, on November 11, 1778, Cherry Valley was the site of a massacre that was led by Mohawk War Chief Joseph Brant. Forty-seven people were killed, thirty-two of whom were noncombatants, and most of them were killed by tomahawk. One of Ogden's sons, David, was killed, and his wife and seven remaining children fled to the woods for safety.

It appears Ogden had an aversion to living too close to others, and it is said that he led a secluded life in Cherry Valley. One historic account says that, on one hunting trip in that area, he came upon another hunter. They sat together talking for a time before Ogden learned that the man lived twelve miles from him. As the story goes, Ogden abruptly left this new acquaintance, went home and told his family they had to pull up stakes, as the neighbors were getting too close. The family moved to Clearfield County after Ogden and his three of his sons scouted out the new region.

When Ogden and his sons arrived in Clearfield County in 1797, they landed about half a mile south of the site that is now the location of the Clearfield County Courthouse, one of the areas where there was evidence of recent cultivation at the site of the Native village of Chinklacamoose. Several meanings have been attached to this Native name, "one, a corruption of the word Achtschingi-clamme, meaning 'it almost joins'—having reference to the stream at this point."[164]

Ogden built a log cabin and returned to Cherry Valley before bringing his family, including his wife and all of his children, Abner, Jonathan, Joab, Jehu, Matthew and Margaret, to Chinklacamoose (Clearfield).[165] Life was difficult. Early settlers had to be innovative, to say the least. With the nearest gristmill located in Lock Haven, a long and difficult trip both ways, Ogden made use of a plane known as a jointer, using the tool to finely chip corn by shoving the ears along the face of the plane. Even the early housewives were innovative, in that Mrs. Ogden used this rough powder to bake bread for the family.

Early settlers in the region did not come because they thought they would become rich. They came for the land. It is apparent, however, that they could not support their families by selling the crops they produced, and for that reason, some, like Ogden, turned to another trade, lumbering. By 1805, Ogden was operating a mill, exporting sawed lumber via the river, which helped him pay off his land.

Daniel Ogden died in 1819.

OLD "UNCLE" BILLY LONG

Bill Long, the King Hunter of Northwestern Pennsylvania. Sketch courtesy of W.J. McKnight's A Pioneer History of Northwestern Pennsylvania *(1905), 150.*

In an area of Pennsylvania where hunting is a sport enjoyed by many, it is interesting to look back to an earlier time to fathom the amount of wildlife that was extant in the region. The Pennsylvania Wilds has a strong tradition of hunting. As a child, I remember hunters from out of the area coming in droves to my hometown of Ridgway in Elk County for the first few days of deer season. Hunting is so ingrained in our psyche that our local schools grant the first day of hunting season as a holiday for students.

In the early days, there were great numbers of game in the woods of the Wilds—beyond anything that we experience now. Just taking a look at the record of William Long provides a snapshot of the hunting trade.

William Long, sometimes referred to as Old "Uncle" Billy Long, enjoyed a reputation as a great hunter. Born near Reading, Pennsylvania (Berks County), about 1794, he was the son of Louis (Ludwig) Long. His mother and father were both German. They settled first in Port Barnett in Jefferson County, and Billy Long eventually lived in Huston Township, Clearfield County, near the present-day village of Penfield.[166] In an article that appeared in the *Clearfield Progress*, a writer explained that, in the early years, professional hunters were "contracted to provide various lumber camps with fresh meat…[and] also killed many kinds of game to be sold and shipped to market."[167] The article noted that Long was the king hunter of Pennsylvania. "He died in 1880, but in his carefully kept game book, the number of bears he killed adds up to the amazing total of 1,500 bruins. Just to complete the record, that game book also shows he had taken 350 elk, 5,000 deer, 100 panthers and 500 wolves in his time."[168]

With accounts of Long being in the region as early as 1815, it is very possible that he was one of the hunters who provided the more settled regions of Pennsylvania with a supply of game in 1816, during the period known as "the year without a summer."

Early Schools

In 1682, William Penn gave his governors and provincial council instruction to "erect and order all publick [*sic*] schools." Nearly one hundred years later, in 1776, a plan or frame of government was introduced "to provide a school or schools in each county for the convenient instruction of youth with such salaries to the masters paid by the public as may enable them to instruct youth at low prices."[169] By 1809, it became the duty of the county commissioners to annually instruct assessors to provide a list of all children between the ages of five and twelve who were unable to pay for schooling.

Early records reveal that the first school in Clearfield County dated back to 1803–4 and was located in a place southwest of Curwensville, which, today, is the site of the McClure Cemetery. According to a newspaper article that was published in 1879, there was no real necessity for schools until the year 1824, as most of the early settlers were men without families. The buildings, which were erected from logs, functioned as both schools and churches.[170]

A schoolmaster's qualifications were "to be able to write, read a little, make quill pens and be able to find the cost of 40 pounds of beef at 2–3 cents per pound and be able to properly apply the birch or witch hazel rod. 'No lickin, no learnin' was then universally believed."[171] Early schoolmasters were Peter Hoover, Reuben Hunter, Daniel Spackman, Whitson Cooper, Samuel Waring, John Patton Sr., James Read, John B. Heisey, Samuel Fulton, Miss Brockway, Eliza Jane Jacobs and Eliza Mapes.

25.
Clinton County

Clinton County was created on June 21, 1839, and was probably named for Governor DeWitt Clinton of New York. The name appears to have been a substitute for the name "Eagle." There were opponents to the formation of the new county, and the name change from "Eagle" to "Clinton" appears to have satisfied those who were against the formation of the county. Its first settlement was established on Great Island by squatters around 1762.[172]

The Legend of Youngwomanstown

At the beginning of the seventeenth century, there were four distinct tribes of Natives living in Pennsylvania. The Delaware, living near the Delaware River; the Susquahannock in the Susquehanna River basin; the Monongahela, living in the upper Ohio River and its tributaries; and the Eries, living south of Lake Erie.[173]

Native society had very definite rules about marriage. Among the Delaware, marriages were arranged by the parents, but the children were not coerced to marry the future mates who were chosen by their parents. Marriage generally took place at the age of seventeen or eighteen for men and at the age of thirteen or fourteen for girls. Any conversations between the intended bride and groom during the period of courtship were chaperoned.

Left: Clinton County Courthouse in Lock Haven, Pennsylvania. *Courtesy of Wikimedia Commons.*

Above: Hyner Run State Park near North Bend (formerly Young Woman's Town). *Courtesy of the Pennsylvania Department of Natural Resources.*

Native men were expected to provide gifts for their future families, "blankets, cloth, linen and a few belts of wampum to the nearest relations of the person he has fixed upon. If they happen to be pleased, both with the present and the character and conduct of the suitor, they propose the matter to the girl, who generally decides agreeably to the wish of her parents and relations.... But if the other party chooses to decline the proposal, they return the present by way of a friendly negative."[174]

Consider, then, the legend that surrounds North Bend, a small village in Clinton County. In the early census records, North Bend was known as Youngwomanstown—yes, written as one word. It took its name from Young Woman's Creek, which enters the West Branch of the Susquehanna River from the north.

Research does not reveal when the legend began, nor which tribe is associated with the legend—the Susquahannock tribe who resided in the Susquehanna River basin in the 1600s, or the Delaware who were pushed further west by encroaching white society in the 1700s.

The legend definitely deals with the decorum that was to be followed in courtship between a Native man and woman.

> *It is said that a young Indian squaw of rare beauty, the hand of whom had been sought by a young chief of another tribe and whose advances had been forbidden by the father of the young girl, and after all efforts on her*

The Legend of Youngwomanstown. Original sketch by Amayah Pollnac.

> *part to soften his feelings towards the young chief had proved ineffectual, she deliberately cast herself into the turbid current near the mouth of the stream and was never more seen.*[175]

It is claimed her ghost can still be seen gliding over the water.

Great Island

Great Island, located near the present-day county seat of Lock Haven, contains 325 acres of land. The soil was so rich that it was a favorite place among the Natives for growing corn. The Munseys, a branch of the Delaware tribe, claimed the island and the country north of the river as their hunting ground.[176] With many paths crossing through the region, it was a major stopping-off point for Natives who were traveling up and down the river. It is known that many councils for peace and war were held by the Natives on the island, and they also met to enjoy sports, amusements and worship the

Great Spirit.[177] There is evidence that there were many burials on the island in a time long before the arrival of the later-known Native tribes.[178]

During the French and Indian War, the French traveled into the area from the Great Lakes in an effort to turn the Indians against the English. By 1756, as the war raged in Pennsylvania, bands of Indians who were living near Great Island were terrorizing settlers. One colonel, John Hambright, along with forty men, was sent from Fort Augusta to "attack, burn and destroy villages" and "kill, scalp and capture" all the Indians they found. With the Natives on Great Island apparently being friendly, their villages were still standing after Hambright's expedition. In 1763, when Colonel John Armstrong made his famous Kittanning Expedition to reclaim captives, as reported in an earlier chapter, his expedition marched through the area and destroyed a village on the island, along with two hundred acres of corn. The Natives never rebuilt their homes and quit gathering at Great Island.[179]

When early surveyors came into the area, a young Irishman named William Dunn was with them. While many stories have been told about Dunn, one that catches the most interest is the account that says he "bought" the island from a Native chief for a barrel of whiskey, a rifle and a hatchet.[180] Dunn was apparently a squatter on the land. In 1784, after the commonwealth purchased the island from the Natives, Dunn made an application for the island and reportedly paid the government "30 pounds per hundred acres or almost $1.50 an acre. This price was said to be the highest ever charged a West Branch settler by the government."[181]

There is a legend, possibly a "myth," that William Penn visited Great Island. The story was related in an article in the *Express* (Lock Haven), with Henry W. Shoemaker listed as its source. Shoemaker was an interesting man, born in New York State, who spent his summers at McElhatten, which greatly influenced his life. Among his many interests was writing about the traditions of the Pennsylvania "mountaineers." In 1924, he cofounded the Pennsylvania Folklore Society and, later, was on the staff of the Pennsylvania Historic and Museum Commission. According to the article, Penn traveled up the West Branch of the Susquehanna in 1701. Shoemaker claimed the story had been handed down by none other than Catherine Smith, the Revolutionary War Patriot who was mentioned in the chapter on Cameron County. She and her husband, Peter Smith, had spent some time at Great Island before settling at White Deer Township around 1770. However, if Catherine Smith was retelling the legend, it was from secondhand information, as she wasn't alive in 1701, when Penn was supposed to have made the trip. It is, however, a good example of the tradition of the mountaineers. The account

Great Island Historic Marker, a Pennsylvania Historic and Museum commission. *Courtesy of Wikimedia Commons.*

begins: "Antoine White, a French Canadian trader, who, as tradition has it, died on Great Island in 1760, claimed he was one of the rowers. Penn traveled from Philadelphia to the Schuylkill in his barge, disembarking at Schuylkill Haven, where he boarded a birch canoe and proceeded down the Swatara River through Jonestown to Middletown, where he was entertained by an Indian chief." Eventually, with a group of French boatmen, they made their way up the Susquehanna River to Great Island, "where there were Indian settlements, Penn was entertained."

> *The great medicine was drunk, wampum belts exchanged and hopakans (pipes of peace) smoked. Penn hunted and fished, catching Susquehanna salmon, herring, muskalong, sturgeons and other fish, which then abounded. He hunted bears, elk, deer and wild turkeys, and shot pelicans, swans and various wild ducks and geese. At the mouth of Deer Creek….NoNeena, a chief's daughter, got in her canoe and accompanied Penn and party to the end of the journey, where the river abruptly ended with a cherry tree, 200 feet high, and roots 20 feet in diameter. Here, the council of chiefs, notified of the coming of Onas, as Penn was called, welcomed him.*[182]

There were great celebrations on Penn's arrival. "Young Secretan was the Indian master of ceremonies, and when Penn arrived, signal fires were blazing, whole elk and bears were being roasted, and the sound of Indian music resounded from every hill."[183] The chief, known as Wi-daagh, took Penn to his spring, a great honor, where only chiefs could drink, "as it banished death and gave certain immortality."[184] At Nippeno Park (Lycoming County), the site is known as "the Widows Spring" today.

William Penn died in England in 1718, more than seventeen years after his supposed visit to Great Island. In 1984, more than three centuries after he founded the colony of Pennsylvania, Penn was made an honorary citizen of the United States.

Cleary Campbell

A look at family trees listed on www.ancestry.com under Cleary Campbell reveals his birthdate as 1740 and place of birth as Ireland. He may be a member of one of those many Irish families who immigrated to Pennsylvania prior to the French and Indian War, as discussed in an earlier chapter about the settlement of Pennsylvania. With the surname Campbell, which has its origins in Scotland, I would venture that he did immigrate from Ireland but was of Scotch-Irish descent (the Scots, known as the Ulster Scots, having settled in Northern Ireland during the reign of James VI of Scotland and England). According to one account, Campbell is a nickname in Gaelic that means "crooked mouth" or "wry-mouthed."[185]

As students walk around the campus of Lock Haven University, it is doubtful they have heard the story of Cleary Campbell, who is credited with being the first settler in what is now known as Clinton County. In 1769, in that period following the years of warfare with the French and Indians, Campbell built a log cabin near the present site of Lock Haven University, apparently squatting on land known as the Charles Glass Tract.[186] There has been speculation as to why Campbell settled in what was then a remote region. Was he another rugged individual who enjoyed the peace that this wild area offered him? It is hard to say. What has been written about him is not very complimentary, the fact being that he "was regarded as the laziest man to be found. The houses of that day were cabins with one room that served for parlor, kitchen and bedroom. It was invariably the practice of Cleary Campbell, being too lazy to sit up, to throw himself down on a bed."[187]

There is more to know about Campbell than his reputation for being lazy. He was married to Anna Gambel on February 23, 1761, at St. James Episcopal Church in Lancaster. Her birth year is also recorded as 1740, so they were both approximately twenty-one years of age when they were married. She would have been with him when he settled in Clinton County. Cleary Campbell served as a lieutenant in the Revolutionary War in James Burd's Battalion of the Northumberland County Militia. Later, he was appointed assessor for Bald Eagle Township, and it is noted that he wrote "in a very plain, good hand."[188] Apparently, he had received more education than many in that era. He, along with John Fleming, was an overseer of the poor.

At one point, Campbell settled on Muncy Mountain (Bald Eagle), near Bellefonte. When he died at the age of eighty-five, he was living near Howard. His wife passed in 1784 at the relatively young age of forty-four. His children were William Campbell, Sarah Delong, Margaret Delong and Allen Campbell.[189]

JEREMIAH CHURCH

Lock Haven lies along the West Branch of the Susquehanna River, on the southern slope of Bald Eagle Mountain. The town is located on the site of a former frontier post, Fort Reed, and was founded on November 4, 1833, by Jeremiah Church, an interesting character.[190] According to an article in the *Express*, when Lock Haven was celebrating the 180th anniversary of its founding, the paper printed that Church had grown up in Bainbridge, New York, and "was thrown out of school at age thirteen for trying to kiss the teacher."[191] Church was a widower, for his wife, Maria, had died soon after the birth of their daughter, Margaret. The author of the *Express* article, while looking though library archives, discovered that Church advertised the creation of a new community. The writer explains, however, that Church didn't "advertise" in newspapers or by street signs. He dropped in at a corner saloon, where he would draw attention to himself by ordering a drink and calling out, "Fraulein, give me a whiskey sour and leave the spoon in it."[192] Once everyone was looking at the man who wanted the spoon left in his drink, he would announce that he wanted to sell lots and create a city.

Church eventually moved away from Lock Haven, but he is remembered today with a plaque that bears his name at Canal Park. Lock Haven was incorporated as a borough in 1840 and as a city in 1870. "It was named for the Pennsylvania Canal Lock and the huge lumber boom that made it a haven for lumberjacks from nearby logging camps."[193]

26.

Elk County

Elk County was formed in 1843 from McKean, Jefferson and Clearfield Counties. An examination of the maps in Paul A.W. Wallace's *Indian Paths of Pennsylvania* identifies the area that we know today as Elk County as being part of the Buffalo Swamp.

An early survey of the region reported that near the Bennett's Branch of the Sinnemahoning River, there was a marsh identified as Flag Swamp, which the writer noted, "In wet seasons, the water flows both ways, and where at such seasons, the summit might easily be passed in a canoe." The writer continues, "This point is remarkable as, probably, the only one in the state where the beaver can be found. Everywhere else, they have been driven out by the approach of human footsteps. In the same region, a few elk still remain."[194]

The following information was written by an early resident of Elk County, John Brooks, a man who certainly had a way with words. It provides a glimpse of early life in the region and the hardships endured by the pioneers.

> *Axes and hoes were clumsily made by the rough blacksmith. Grain and hay were stacked in the fields or yard or put into round log barns. Threshing was done with flail, or trampled out with oxen or horses; the grain was separated from the chaff by winnowing it through the meshes of a riddle, made for the purpose, while the breezes would carry away the chaff; or in a clam, two persons would raise and maintain a blast by a dexterous swinging movement of a double linen bed sheet, while the third person*

Elk County Courthouse in Ridgway, Pennsylvania. *Courtesy of John Myers.*

> *would winnow the threshed grain from the riddle. Corn and buckwheat were sometimes ground on hand-mills and sifted through sieves made from dressed perforated sheep or deer skins, drawn over a wide oaken hoop.*[195]

And the women worked alongside the men.

> *Native forest fruit was then abundant…game was plenty, the rivers were streams of crystal liquid. Women frequently performed a part of the farm service in that age, some with sickle and rake in hand, doing the work of a harvest man. Others, with hoe and fork, did good work in the hay and corn field. One of them is remembered as placing her child in a sap-trough nearby when but little over a week old while she split more rails in a day than her husband.*[196]

WAPITI

What's in a name? "Many biologists believe the name wapiti (WAA-pi-tea) is a Shawnee Indian word meaning 'white rump,' an appropriate description for the elk's large rump patch."[197] Eastern elk once roamed the Commonwealth of Pennsylvania, with vast herds being found from northern New York to Central Georgia. Pennsylvania's largest concentration of elk was believed to have been in the Allegheny Mountains. Colonization led to their demise, as elk were pursued wherever they were found.[198]

By the mid-1860s, a few native elk were still roaming in Pennsylvania's Elk and Cameron Counties. Gone were the vast herds that trampled the ground

Right: Two Bull Elk Shedding Their Velvet. Courtesy of Paul Staniszewski.

Below: Two Bull Elk Sparring During the Annual Fall Mating Ritual Known as the "Rut." Courtesy of Paul Staniszewski.

around the naturally occurring salt licks in their "quest to lick the salt."[199] The last two reports of elk being hunted in Pennsylvania include one that was taken not far from St. Marys in Elk County by an Indian named Jim Jacobs in the 1860s and a second taken by a hunter named John Decker in Centre County in 1877.

Elk are much larger than whitetail deer; a male elk, with his massive, spreading antlers, can weigh between six hundred and one thousand pounds. Females are about 25 percent smaller.[200] A man by the name of Ernest Thompson Seton wrote extensively about North American elk in his book *Lives of Game Animals*, which was published in 1909.

> *There are few stories of blood lust more disgusting than that detailing the slaughter of the great Elk bands. The deer of New England were killed off for the meat. But the wholesale massacre of the elk, like that of the buffalo, was carried on for the joy of seeing the great creatures fall in dying agony; and, in later years, by tusk hunters who were too lazy to be hide hunters.... The beginning of the nineteenth century saw the wapiti perfectly described, catalogued, and started on the road to extermination. Thenceforth, travelers in eastern America were obliged to record only the reminiscences of old settlers or the discovery of fossil horns and skulls.*[201]

The Pennsylvania Game Commission was established in 1895. In 1912, Joseph Kalbfus, the agency's executive secretary, spoke about the possibility of reintroducing elk to Pennsylvania. This idea stemmed from a report that said, in Yellowstone National Park and the Jackson Hole Refuge Area, the herds of elk had increased to such a point that biologists, who were responsible for protecting the remnants of the elk population, had come up with a plan to relocate some of the herd while trying to feed those remaining elk through the winter months. In 1913, Pennsylvania received its first shipment of Yellowstone elk by train. The fifty elk cost about thirty dollars each. Half of them went to Clinton County, the other half to Clearfield County. Later in the year, twenty-two elk were brought in and released on state lands in Monroe County; the remainder were released at a Centre County preserve.[202]

The elk were brought into the region by boxcar and chased into the Wilds, a terrain much different than the one they were accustomed to in Yellowstone. A newspaper article printed in the *Harrisburg Daily Independent* in April 1913 noted:

> *The Yellowstone Park elk brought into the state by the State Game Commission and sent to forestry reservations in Clearfield and Clinton Counties, are not doing as well as could be expected. Seven of them have died since being brought here, five in Clinton and two in Clearfield county. Their deaths are accounted for in the moist climate. Elk are used to the high altitudes in the cold, dry air, and they were not acclimated to the moist atmosphere of Pennsylvania; consequently, they were very susceptible to pulmonary disease and some of them succumbed. The State Game Commission has hopes of saving the others, and they are being very carefully looked after by the game warden.*[203]

According to the game commission, when the elk were released, they began to wander in search of food and cover, and "within a week, some had traveled as far as forty miles away from the release sites."[204]

While many were in favor of the elk program, the animals were destructive in farming areas. Illegal harvests by poachers and farmers, as well as those who wanted to hunt them, were not uncommon. "In 1913, the Pennsylvania General Assembly enacted a law protecting them until November 1921, when a two-week elk season would be held. Bulls with at least four points to one antler were identified in the law as legal game for the distant season."[205]

Two Bull Elk Sparring During the "Rut." Courtesy of Paul Staniszewski.

Bull and Cow Elk. Courtesy of Paul Staniszewski.

In a 1970 article in the *Progress* (Clearfield, Pennsylvania), it was stated that the elk became so abundant that, from 1923 to 1932, an open season was held to hunt them. Since that time, the elk have been protected. In that same 1970 article, a ten-point program was developed for consideration by state agencies. Noting that the elk range encompassed about 10,560 acres owned by the game commission and various other organizations, it was proposed that all the land in question could be acquired by direct purchase or exchange by the game commission. The proposal set boundaries for special elk management areas, with rules and regulations regarding public use. The plan discussed elk management, construction of all-weather roads for public access into the management areas and the prohibition of certain vehicles, among other specific regulations relating to the herd.[206]

With what seems to have been an ambitious plan, strides have been made to provide habitat for the elk.

> *Over the past two decades, the Pennsylvania Game Commission, the Pennsylvania Department of Conservation and Natural Resources, the Keystone Elk Country Alliance and other organizations have worked to conserve and protect elk and their habitat. Through improvements in the elk range and other efforts, it is hoped this wonderful animal will continue to roam the Pennsylvania Wilds.*[207]

Benezette, Winslow Hill and Elk Country

The area known as Winslow Hill, where the Elk Country Visitor Center stands today, is located in Benezette Township, just outside of the village of Benezette. There is local lore concerning how the name Benezette came to be. Said to have been retold in a local newspaper in 1895, the story is as follows:

> *Long ago, when the Indians were still there, a white family lived where the town now stands. The white family had a little boy named Bennie, and Bennie went into the woods and got lost. Everyone hunted for Bennie—even the Indians helped, but the child could not be found. One Indian, looking very sad, said to the father and mother, "Bennies et" (meaning a bear had eaten Bennie). Repeating it many times to all who gathered, it soon became "Bennieset or Benezett."*[208]

Left: *Rebecca Hicks Winslow*, the great granddaughter of White Indian Levi Hicks. *Courtesy of Kathy Myers.*

Middle: *Homestead of Charles and Rebecca Hicks Winslow, Winslow Hill, Benezette. Courtesy of Kathy Myers.*

Bottom: *Elk County Visitor Center. Courtesy of www.elkcountryvisitorcenter.com.*

There are reports of a John Bennett, born in Lycoming County, arriving in the region with his father in 1787 to hunt beaver. After building a cabin near the village of Caledonia, they were in the region until 1796—a reference having been made to their cabin by an early surveyor in 1794. It is likely Benezette was named in honor of the Bennett family.

By 1811, handbills had been distributed, advertising that 140,000 acres of land would be sold in McKean and Clearfield Counties (at that time, Elk County was part of Clearfield County). "These hand bills were dated Burlington, New Jersey, December 16, 1811, and were signed by Coxe, McMurtie, Shippen Cox. The land was to be sold to 'actual settlers' at 'two dollars per acre on five-year credit—two years without interest.'"[209]

In 1818, Carpenter and Elizabeth Colburn Winslow, along with their extended family, emigrated from Maine to Pennsylvania, settling in an area just outside of Punxsutawney. In 1823, three of the Winslow brothers, Carpenter Jr., Reuben Colburn and Ebenezer, moved on to Elk County. Reuben is credited with founding the village of Benezette, which is situated at the base of Winslow Hill. George Winslow, the son of Carpenter Jr. and Beulah Keene Winslow, is recognized as the person who named Winslow Hill. In the early years of settlement, it was best known for farming. Eventually, it grew into a community of approximately one hundred people, with its own school and Methodist church.

Today, descendants of the early families still inhabit the region, although the family farms have mostly disappeared. The Elk Country Visitor Center is located just down the road from the one of the Winslow homes which is still standing. Built by Charles and Rebecca Hicks Winslow in 1845, Rebecca Hicks Winslow was the great-granddaughter of White Indian Levi Hicks, who was captured at the Great Cove Massacre in 1755 and killed by Indians at Spruce Creek in 1778, during the Great Runaway.

The Kersey Road

The Village of Kersey is situated in Elk County, not far from the City of St. Marys. What many may not know about Kersey (formerly known as Centerville) is that there was a main path known as the Kersey Road that brought the early settlers into the region.

In August 1929, the *Courier-Express* (DuBois, Pennsylvania) interviewed the elderly ninety-three-year-old George C. Kirk Esq., who discussed his career as a land surveyor, which took him all through Clearfield County, into Jefferson County and Elk County, as well as other locations in Pennsylvania. In addition to his surveying skills, Mr. Kirk had a great interest in the early history of Clearfield County and wrote a manuscript, *Pioneer Days in Brady Township*, that was placed in the DuBois Public Library and also ran as a series in the *Courier-Express*.

In recalling those past years, Mr. Kirk referred to an old Native Trail that became known as the Kersey Road. He related the history of the construction of the road from 1810:

> *Fox, Norris and company, wealthy Friends of Philadelphia, came into possession of about 140,000 acres of land…situated and lying at that time in Clearfield and McKean Counties, respectively, and was taken into Elk County when that county was organized in 1843. These people employed a man by the name of William Kersey, under a power of attorney, as their agent, to build a saw and gristmills, and make such other necessary improvements as to him shall seem advisable and for the improvement of their property. Under this power of attorney, he was also to construct a road into their lands, from some point on the old state highway, to any place on Elk Creek that he would select, on which to build the mills.*[210]

The site selected by Kersey was an Indian path that branched off of the Great Shamokin Path.

Interestingly, when Kersey arrived in 1811 with a crew of men and implements to build the road, he selected a point "on the old state highway, about four and one-half miles, eastward from where the Village of Luthersburg is now located." Kirk related:

> [This road], *as laid out and constructed by Mr. Kersey…followed the old Indian trail, passing through unbroken forest of virgin timber, where the ravages of the white man's axe had never before felled those beautiful monarchs of the forest, and laid the corner stone for the foundation for its destruction; continuing on over Boons Mountain, crossing Little Toby Creek, near where Hellen Mills; from thence, it followed up the creek to the point of "Hogback" Hill, up which it went through very steep and difficult to ascent in many places; thence, the road continued over the high and hill ground to the place Kersey had selected for his millsite on Elk Creek.*[211]

Top: Summit of Boone's Mountain, Route 153, Following the Old Kersey Road, Looking North Toward Helen's Mills on Route 219. Courtesy of John Myers.

Middle: Approaching the Summit of Boone's Mountain from the South, on Route 153. Courtesy of John Myers.

Bottom: Mountain Laurel, the State Flower of Pennsylvania. Courtesy of Wikimedia Commons.

Some of the early settlers in the region where Kersey started his mill were Amos Davis, John Kyler, Elijah Meredith, Jacob Wilson, Jonah Griffith and Samuel Miller.[212] Between 1817 and 1823, many others settled in the region, thanks, in part, to the road built by Kersey following the old Indian path.

Boone's Mountain, today, remains a wild area in the region. In 1966–67, a new paved road was opened, replacing the dirt road that crossed the mountain, sometimes varying from the established route. I can imagine that parts of the old dirt road closely followed the Indian path across the mountain. Part of PA Route 153, it intersects with PA Route 219 just north of the old Helen's Mills intersection.

> *Boone's Mountain reaches a height of two thousand two hundred sixty-five feet.…Stone and sand were both quarried.…Mountain laurel, once flourished here.…Wild grape vines and some hazel nut trees remain.… If one is searching for wild flowers, a person might come across trailing arbutus, wood anemone, bloodroot, bluebells, buttercups, wild honeysuckle, Dutchman's Britches, Jack-in-the-Pulpit, Lady's Slipper, Mandrake, wild lily of the valley, mustard, painted trillium and violets.*[213]

27.

Jefferson County

Come for fun, stay for good! It is a great place to live, work, raise a family and enjoy the outdoors.[214]

Jefferson County came into existence by an act of assembly passed March 26, 1804; it was formed from parts of Lycoming, Huntingdon and Somerset Counties. The same act placed it under the jurisdiction of Westmoreland County until 1806, when it was placed under the jurisdiction of Indiana County. In 1830, Jefferson County attained full jurisdiction over its own affairs.[215] "Previous to the War of 1812, there were no roads; the 'Chinklacamoose Path' from Clearfield through Punxsutawney, and 'Meade's Trail' from Clearfield through Brookville westward were the only highways."[216]

Joseph Barnett

Joseph Barnett is credited with being the first settler in Jefferson County. Barnett was born in Dauphin County in 1754 and was of Scotch-Irish descent. His father, a farmer, was a native of Ireland who immigrated to Pennsylvania in the early part of the eighteenth century.[217] Barnett's mother died when he was young, and he was brought up by relatives on a farm. A Patriot of the Revolution, he served in the state militia in

Jefferson County Courthouse, Brookville, Pennsylvania. Courtesy of Wikimedia Commons.

the campaign against the Wyoming Boys. After the war, he settled in Northumberland County but lost the land due to a problem with the title.[218] "The Record of the Burial Place of Veteran, Joseph Barnett," lists his Revolutionary service as being with the Northumberland County Militia, First Company, Fourth Battallion; date of service September 26, 1776–unknown; rank, private.

Barnett arrived in Jefferson County with his brother, Andrew Barnett, and Samuel Scott from Lycoming County in 1795. Settling on the confluence of Mill Creek and Sandy Lick Creek, they named the site Port Barnett. They began by erecting a sawmill on Mill Creek. Joseph Barnett returned to his family in the fall of that year. While Andrew Barnett and Scott were left to finish some work, Barnett became ill and died. Only Scott and two Natives who were helping them build the mill attended his funeral, and he was buried on the north bank, where the two creeks merged.[219]

Scott, who was Joseph Barnett's brother-in-law, soon returned to Lycoming County with the news. In the following year, 1796, Joseph Barnett and Scott returned, accompanied by a young man names Moses Knapp, to finish their work. With the mill finished, some lumber was sawed, and plans were made for a permanent settlement.[220]

In the spring of 1797, Joseph Barnett brought his wife, Elizabeth, and his twin children, Thomas and Sarah, to their wilderness home. The first white child born in Jefferson County was J.P. Barnett, and the first white female child born in the county was Rebecca Barnett. The Barnett's were the parents of ten children, all of whom, except for Thomas and Sarah, were born in the county.[221]

It has often been said that necessity is the mother of invention. As Barnett had to travel on an Indian trail, with "only blazes on the tree to guide him, and the stars by night," he once carried sixty pounds of flour on his back from Pittsburgh to his home. His usual method of travel was a raft of sawed lumber, which he took to Pittsburgh in the spring, when the water was high. Taking a canoe along, on the return trip, it would be loaded with what the family needed. Using poles to push the canoe up the Allegheny River to Red Bank Creek, supplies were then brought to Port Barnett. Around 1801, Barnett put up a small gristmill using native stones for "buhrs," one of the projections that resembles teeth on such a stone. His mill was used for several years by settlers and the Natives, who also brought in corn they had grown.[222] Life was made a little easier through Joseph Barnett's improvement.

In addition to running the gristmill, Barnett ran a sawmill and rafted lumber on Sandy Lick and Red Bank Creek. He became postmaster at Port Barnett in 1826.[223]

Jefferson County's first settler died at his home, where he had lived for forty-one years, on April 15, 1838. His wife, Elizabeth, soon followed, passing away just four months after his death. He was eighty-four years old at the time, and his wife was sixty-five.[224]

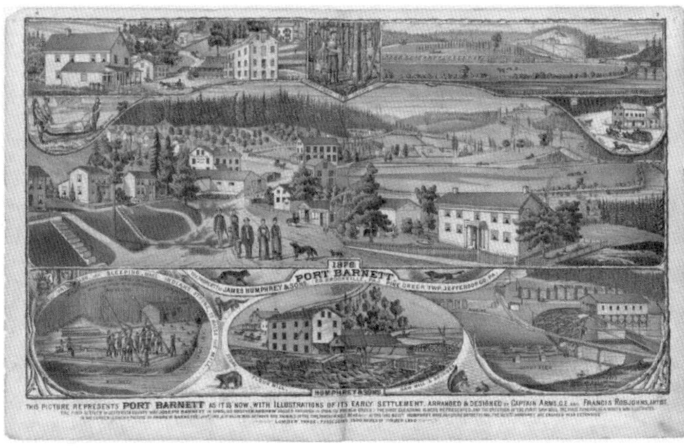

Port Barnett, Founded by Early Jefferson County Settler, Joseph Barnett, a print found in Caldwell's *Illustrated Historical Combination Atlas of Jefferson County, Pennsylvania. Courtesy of the Library of Congress.*

SARAH BARNETT GRAHAM

The story of Sarah Barnett Graham is fascinating. When her father, Joseph Barnett, brought his family into the wilderness, Sarah and her twin brother, Thomas, were seven years old. They were born in Lycoming County in 1790, while their father was operating a sawmill there. In her own words, Sarah recounted the following:

> *Now, reader, as I have stated, I was seven years old when I came to this county, you will find that I have lived eighty years in the county. I have seen the Indian give way to the white man, the pack-horse to the wagon, and the wagon to the railroad. I remember the screams of the panther, and the howl of the wolf as things of the past, and in a few years more, I will, as they, be gone forever.*[225]

Life was not easy in the wilderness. One of the early Jefferson County inhabitants recalled living for a week on dried apples and cornbread. Having white wheat cakes at Christmas was a great treat. Another local remembered when their family was so short on food, they boiled pumpkin seeds; while another family lived on green corn for two weeks.[226] The nearest settlements in which to buy supplies were more than forty or fifty miles away.

Children had their chores in those years, and Sarah Barnett was no exception. She recalled a time when she was about fourteen years old and was sent out to bring the cows in one evening. The cows had strayed farther than usual. Before she found them, it was night, and a thunderstorm was brewing. Becoming frightened, Sarah lost her way. In an era when wolves roamed the woods, Sarah worried that the wolves might be stalking her, and she was afraid to stop in the dense forest. Making her way to Mill Creek, she waded out to the middle and climbed on a large rock, where she spent the night in terror. Hearing the calls of those searching for her, she mistakenly thought the calls and the barking dogs were the howling of the wolves, so she stayed put. When she was finally rescued at daylight, the water was rapidly rising, and by noon, the rock that had been her refuge was completely covered by Mill Creek. She notes that she was never sent to hunt the cows again but said that if her father had instructed her to do so, she would have done his bidding in spite of her fear. While Mr. Barnett was known for his kindness to his family, he was also a strict disciplinarian, and his children did not disobey him.[227]

Elisha Graham, born in Dauphin County in 1772, arrived in Port Barnett in 1804; once there, he went to work for Joseph Barnett. Elisha was the son of another Patriot of the Revolution, John Graham, who was born in Scotland to John Graham and an heiress named Janet Caldwell. Young John was fascinated with the accounts he heard of the New World and immigrated to the "Land of Penn," settling on a farm in Dauphin County. Eventually, he married Martha Miller.[228] After enlisting in the army during the Revolution, he fought in a number of battles before he was captured by the British near Long Island. Held as a prisoner for two years in New York City, the British agents promised him a pardon and reward if he renounced his American sentiments and fought for the king. Rejecting their offer, he remained in jail but was eventually pardoned and returned to his home.[229]

While John was away, the Great Runaway of 1778 forced his wife and children, including Elisha, to escape with other settlers. Making a trip down the Susquehanna River in a canoe, Mrs. Graham placed her children and all she could bring with her in a canoe. As fate would have it, the canoe was upset, and all the contents were lost in the river. The mother and children all survived. One item rescued by Mrs. Graham was an early publication of the Bible, which was handed down through the family. This remarkable woman, who struggled alone with her children in the Susquehanna River, became Sarah Barnett's mother-in-law.[230]

In 1807, Sarah Barnett married Elisha Graham. In 1821, after they had been married for fourteen years, the couple moved to a farm in Union Township, remaining there until 1830, when they relocated to Eldred Township. Mr. Graham served as a clerk for the first board of Jefferson County Commissioners and as a court crier for several years. He died in 1854. The 1850 Federal Census lists the members of the household as Elijah Graham, Sarah Graham, John Graham, Eliza Graham, Isaiah Graham, Milton Graham and Beatrice Preston.

Elisha Graham's widow survived him until October 1885, when she died at the age of ninety-five.[231] It was a remarkable lifespan in a time when life expectancy for the white population ranged from around thirty-eight to forty years of age.

CARPENTER AND ELIZABETH COLBURN WINSLOW

Was it the year without a summer or the offering of land by the Holland Land Company's advertisement that induced Carpenter and Elizabeth Colburn Winslow to enter Pennsylvania with their extended family around 1818?

Carpenter Winslow was born on March 22, 1766, in Pittston, Maine, the son of James and Anna Huston Winslow. His father was a millwright, and Carpenter, early in life, became familiar with the use of mechanical implements and, subsequently, engaged in shipbuilding, running a shipyard in Wiscasset, Maine, for some years. He married Elizabeth Colburn in 1787, and they were the parents of nine sons, four of whom became distinguished seamen.[232]

Elizabeth Colburn was the daughter of Major Reuben Colburn, a Patriot of the American Revolution. In 1775, Colburn, another shipbuilder who was living in Pittston, Maine, at the order of George Washington, built two hundred boats for Benedict Arnold's raid into Canada known as the Arnold Expedition. It should be noted that, in addition to building the boats, Colburn rendered other services and never received compensation from the government for those services.[233]

Carpenter's father, James, was a member of the Society of Friends, more commonly known as Quakers, and for that reason, he refused to serve in the Revolution.[234] In spite of his religious beliefs, he and his son, Jonathan, made fifty paddles for the Arnold Expedition into Canada, and for Carpenter's future father-in-law, Reuben Colburn.

An event during the Revolution involving Mrs. James Winslow, Carpenter's mother, serves as a reminder of why we have a Constitution in this country spelling out our rights. Under the Fourth Amendment to the Constitution, "The right of the people to be secure in their persons, houses, papers, and effects, against unreasonable searches and seizures, shall not be violated, and no warrants shall issue, but upon probable cause, supported by oath or affirmation, and particularly describing the place to be searched, and the persons or things to be seized."[235] In 1778–79, "A British scouting party of six entered [Mrs. Winslow's] home and demanded food. Mrs. Winslow said she had nothing cooked. Their reply, 'Boil us hasty pudding, or we will shoot you.' She obeyed the order, and soon, the party was alarmed by an unwonted noise without, and decamped, leaving a silver sword."[236] The sword was eventually passed down to a great-granddaughter. With Carpenter Winslow being about ten years old at the time of that event, it apparently made a lasting

Major Reuben Colburn House, Pittston, Maine, National Register of Historic Places. Courtesy of Wikimedia Commons.

impression on him. As an adult, he received a commission as a lieutenant from Samuel Adams on November 1, 1796.

Out of Winslow's nine sons, four were sea captains, and they did not emigrate to Pennsylvania with their parents. In his fifty-second year, Carpenter, along with his wife, Betsy, and their sons (Carpenter Jr., approximately twenty-five years old with his wife and two children; Reuben, twenty-two years of age; James, twenty years old, along with his wife; Ebenezer, eighteen years old; and Joseph Wood, fourteen years old), made his way to Gaskill Township outside of Punxsutawney, traveling by boat from Maine to the Chesapeake Bay, where they followed the Susquehanna River to the West Branch of the Susquehanna, eventually making their way to Clearfield. The journey continued overland through that part of the Great Shamokin Path that crossed through the Punxsutawney area.[237]

Looking back at the home where Elizabeth Colburn Winslow had lived as a child brings a realization of what she and her extended family were faced with when they arrived in the region, i.e., life in a log cabin. One historian described their life in the wilderness:

Log Cabin from the 1800s Was Placed on the Grounds of the Cathedral of Learning at the University of Pittsburgh to Celebrate Pittsburgh's Bicentennial. Courtesy of Wikimedia Commons.

> *When they came to Jefferson County and settled on what is now the old homestead in Gaskill Township, the country, for many miles around, was an unbroken wilderness, abounding game of all kinds common to that latitude. Like the pioneers of all new countries, they suffered many hardships and great inconveniences, having to pack their grain on horseback from fifteen to twenty miles along bridle paths to mill. But the climate being healthy and the soil productive, they were able to raise an abundance of grain and feed, while the surrounding forests afforded a supply of the choicest game.*[238]

Three of the sons, Carpenter Jr., Reuben and Ebenezer, moved to Elk County around 1823. James Winslow became a Jefferson County surveyor and was also known as a house joiner. Joseph Wood Winslow was a farmer in Gaskill Township, just outside of Punxsutawney, where he resided on the original homestead. Joseph Wood Winslow's son, Reuben Colburn Winslow, was born in 1833 and read law with P.W. Jenks of Punxsutawney. He was later admitted to the bar of Jefferson County. In

Left: *Joseph Winslow Farm*, a print found in Caldwell's *Illustrated Historical Combination Atlas of Jefferson County, Pennsylvania. Courtesy of the Library of Congress.*

Right: *R.C. Winslow Home*, a print found in Caldwell's *Illustrated Historical Combination Atlas of Jefferson County, Pennsylvania. Courtesy of the Library of Congress.*

1884, Reuben Colburn Winslow was elected to the Pennsylvania State Senate, representing the Thirty-Seventh Senatorial District composed of Indiana and Jefferson Counties.[239]

As depicted in prints in Caldwell's 1878 *Atlas of Jefferson County, Pennsylvania*, the family became well-established and prosperous in the Punxsutawney region. The homes depicted in those prints are still in existence today.

Carpenter Winslow died in 1827, and Elizabeth (Betsy) Colburn Winslow died in 1845. Both were buried in the old North Findley Street Cemetery in Punxsutawney, which has recently received the attention of a local group of volunteers who developed a plan to preserve the historic cemetery that was the burial place of many original settlers. The group is known as the North Findley Street Cemetery Guild (NFSCG).

28.
Warren County

Cornplanter, a Seneca Chief

Cornplanter was a warrior on the side of the French during the French and Indian War and was present at the defeat of General Braddock. Although he thought the Indians should not participate in the white man's battles, he eventually joined forces with the British during the Revolutionary War. After a fierce battle in 1779 with Captain Samuel Brady near the mouth of Redbank Creek, Clarion County, which cost the lives of many of his men, he became a peacemaker and signed a treaty with the "Great Chief of the Thirteen Fires" (George Washington) in 1791.

Cornplanter was born around 1732 and lived until 1836, passing from the scene at the age of 104. His Native name was Gyantwachia, "the planter," (also written as Gyantwachia and Gar-yan-wah-ga). Born in Conawaugus on the Genesee River in New York, he was the son of John Abeel, a Dutch trader, and a Seneca woman of chiefly lineage. Historians speculate that his father married his mother to gain the friendship of the Natives, which would have been beneficial in trading with them.

Some historians claim that Cornplanter's white father was abusive to his wife. A different image appears in a letter written by Cornplanter to the governor of Pennsylvania; it seems he barely knew his father.

> *When I was a child, I played with the butterfly, the grasshopper, and the frogs; and as I grew up, I began to pay some attention and play with the*

Warren County Courthouse, Warren, Pennsylvania. Courtesy of Wikimedia Commons.

Indian boys in the neighborhood, and they took notice of my skin being of a different color from theirs, and spoke about it. I inquired from my mother the cause, and she told me my father was a resident of Albany. I still ate my victuals out of a bark dish. I grew up to be a young man and married a wife, and I had no kettle or gun. I then knew where my father lived, and went to see him, and found he was a white man and spoke the English

> *language. He gave me victuals while I was at his house, but when I started to return home, he gave me no provisions to eat on the way. He gave me neither kettle nor gun.*[240]

Cornplanter's reported encounter with his father later in life provides a glimpse into the character of this famous chief, as well as the respect Natives held for their families. When the Seneca were sweeping through the Schoharie and Mohawk Valleys in 1779, Cornplanter took his father prisoner without letting him know who he was. Marching the old man ten or twelve miles, Cornplanter finally confronted him:

> *My name is John O'Bail* [Abeel], *commonly called Cornplanter. I am your son. You are my father. You are now my prisoner and subject to the custom of Indian warfare; but you shall not be harmed. You need not fear. I am a warrior. Many are the scalps which I have taken. Many prisoners have I tortured to death. I am your son. I was anxious to see you and greet you in friendship. I went to your cabin and took you by force; but your life shall be spared. Indians love their friends and their kindred and treat them with kindness. If you now choose to follow the fortunes of your yellow son and to live with our people, I will cherish your old age with plenty of venison, and you shall live easy. But if it is your choice to return to your fields and live with your white children, I will send a party of trusty young men to conduct you back in safety. I respect you, my father. You have been friendly to Indians, and they are your friends.*[241]

His father chose to return to his white family.

Prior to his treaty with the Americans, Cornplanter traveled to Philadelphia to meet with President George Washington and Pennsylvania governor Thomas Mifflin to protest the treatment of his people. A successful visit, he came away with an agreement from Washington and Mifflin to protect his land. Further, in response to Cornplanter's influence in bringing about a lasting peace on the Pennsylvania frontier following the Revolutionary War, the Pennsylvania legislature granted him 1,500 acres of former Seneca territory in Pennsylvania in 1796 for "him and his heirs forever"; this became known as the Cornplanter Tract. One tract, Richland, near West Hickory, was sold to his friend General John Wilkins Jr. Another, labeled the "Gift," was sold in 1818; for this, unfortunately, he received worthless money and notes. The third tract comprised 600 acres, most of it on the west bank of the Allegheny River, just south of the New

Cornplanter, Seneca Chief, a 1796 print from F. Bartoli. *Courtesy of the National Anthropological Archives, Smithsonian Institution.*

York state line (Warren County), and it included his own town, Jenuchshadega, and two islands in the river.

In the years following the peace, Cornplanter was faced with the reality of dealing with an influx of settlers into the region that had been Seneca territory. He made trips to various cities to strengthen relationships between the Natives and white settlers and to learn more about the "European" way of life. He understood the importance of teaching his people new skills when they could no longer rely on hunting or the fur trade as their way of life. He met and admired those of the Quaker faith, and in 1798, he brought in Quaker teachers, established schools, built roads and houses, developed agriculture and bred large herds of cattle. Eventually, they also engaged in cutting and rafting timber.[242]

It seems that Cornplanter's Native name, Gyantwachia, which translates to "the planter," was an appropriate depiction of the famous chief. The Seneca were planters of acres of corn. In 1779, when Colonel Daniel Broadhead led an attack of six hundred men north from Fort Pitt, into what is now Warren County, it was reported that the force burned Cornplanter's town, destroying five hundred acres of corn. General Sullivan, in his march across New York State, reported that Indian storehouses, full of corn and vegetables, were burned. "The corn already destroyed by our Army is not less than 5,000 bushels, upon a modest calculation."[243] It has actually been calculated as 160,000 bushels.[244]

The crop that we call corn was known as maize to the early settlers. It comes from the Native word *mahiz*, which means "that which sustains us," showing its importance to the Natives.[245] "Archaeological and paleobotanical discoveries provide evidence that cultivated corn existed in the southwestern U.S. for at least 3,000 years. Discoveries in the Tehuacan Valley of southern Mexico yielded evidence that wild corn existed there from 5,000 to 3,400 BC."[246] As to the cultivation of corn, "archaeological evidence of corn's early presence in the western hemisphere was identified from corn pollen grain considered to be 80,000 years old 'obtained from drill cores 200 feet below Mexico City.'"[247] It was a well-known crop among the Natives long before Europeans reached this continent. Spread through North America, along the various trade routes of rivers and trails traveled by the Natives, some speculate that "cultivating corn is responsible for turning the Native American tribes from nomadic to agrarian societies."[248] To the Native Americans, "corn was of divine origin—it was the food of the gods that created the earth."[249]

Cornplanter knew well the traditions of his people, including the legends of corn. When the Holland Land Company began to acquire patents to land in the region where Cornplanter resided, one of its workers befriended him, and over a period of time, Cornplanter spoke to him about his memories and told Iroquois legends. The engineer kept notes of the stories, which were eventually acquired and turned into a small book titled *The Legends of the Iroquois: Told by "The Cornplanter."* One of the corn legends is printed here:

> *Long and earnestly, a young brave wooed a beautiful maiden, and at last gained her consent to live with him in his wigwam. But the days and nights were lonely without her, and the young brave could not remain away from her lodge. Fearing that she might be stolen by one of her many admirers, or that danger might come to her, he slept at night in the forest that he might be near to protect her. One night, he was awakened by a light footstep, and, starting up, saw his loved one stealing out of her lodge as a sleepwalker. He pursued her, but, as if fleeing in her dreams from a danger that threatened her life, she ran from him, speeding through the paths like the fleet-footed hare. On and on he followed, and finally, drew so near that he could hear her quick breath and the rapid beating of her heart. With all his remaining strength, the lover sprang forward and clasped the maiden's form to his breast. What was his grief and astonishment when he found that his arms clasped, not the maiden he loved, but a strange plant the like of which he had never seen before. The maiden had awakened just as her lover overtook her and had been so frightened at her surroundings that she was transformed. She had raised her arms to her head just as her lover caught her, and her uplifted hands were changed into ears of corn, and where her fingers caught her hair, the maize bears beautiful silken threads.*[250]

Cornplanter fathered two children, Henry Abeele and Edward Cornplanter. Prior to his death, he made known his wishes—specifically, that his grave would be unmarked. In 1866, the Pennsylvania legislature erected a monument to him:

The Legend of the Corn. Original sketch by Amayah Pollnac.

> *Gy-ant-wa-chia, The Cornplanter,*
> *John O'Bail, Alias Cornplanter,*
> *DIED*
> *At Cornplanter Town, Feb. 18, A.D. 1836,*
> *Aged about 100 years*[251]

Noted on the west side of the stone:

> *Chief of the Seneca tribe, and a principal chief of the Six Nations from the period of the Revolutionary War to the time of his death. Distinguished for talent, courage, eloquence, sobriety, and love for tribe and race, to whose welfare he devoted his time, his energy and his means during a long and eventful life.*[252]

Jesse Cornplanter, the last known direct heir of Cornplanter, died in 1957.[253] It appears that the land designated to "him and his heirs forever," reverted back to the federal government following the death of Jesse Cornplanter.

On St. Patrick's Day, March 17, 1936, extensive flooding occurred in western Pennsylvania. Heavy snowfall that year in northwestern Pennsylvania, combined with warm weather in March and steady rain, sent rivers and creeks over their banks in many western Pennsylvania communities. Pittsburgh was particularly hard hit, as weather observers predicted the worst flood in twelve years there, where the waters from the Allegheny and Monongahela Rivers join to form the Ohio River.[254] "By the time the waters receded a week later, the destruction and devastation was almost unfathomable—62 dead in the region, over 500 injured, 135,000 homeless, and millions of dollars in property damage to homes, businesses and industries."[255] The Flood Control Acts of 1936 and 1938 resulted in a dam that was to be constructed on the Allegheny River in Warren, Pennsylvania.

With its construction started in 1960, the Kinzua Dam was completed in 1965; it encompasses ten thousand acres or one-third of the Seneca Nation's territory, including the acreage that was reserved by Cornplanter. In order to build the dam, a historic Native cemetery was moved. It included the remains of Cornplanter and three hundred of his descendants and followers, including the memorial monument that had been erected in 1866. The dam, which was built primarily for flood control, is also said to be for drought control, recreation and to provide hydroelectric power, which furnishes power for Pittsburgh. The Seneca fought against the construction of the dam but lost. President John F. Kennedy allowed the project to go forward during the term of Pennsylvania governor David Lawrence. To the Seneca, the dam is known as the Lake of Betrayal.

CELERON

Celeron's full name was Pierre Joseph Celeron de Blainville; he was born in 1693 and died in 1759 in Montreal. Many today don't realize the extent to which the French pushed into this region of Pennsylvania and made connections with the Wilds. Celeron de Blainville's presence in Warren County demonstrates the interest of the French in Colonial America and their efforts to control the Indians and oust the British from the New World, particularly from the Ohio Valley.

Celeron, as he is commonly known in this region, was first appointed as a lieutenant commandant to a post in Michilimackinac in 1734; then as a commander at Fort Niagara in Detroit; and, eventually, in 1746, to Fort St. Frederic on Lake Champlain.[256]

In 1748, the governor of Canada ordered Celeron to strengthen the French claim in the Ohio Valley. Setting out from Montreal on June 15, 1749, in a flotilla of large boats and canoes, the expedition included 216 French Canadians and 55 Indians. At the mouth of Chautauqua Creek in what is, today, Westfield, New York, the expedition cut a road over the French Portage Road and carried its boats and equipment overland to Chautauqua

West Hickory Creek Entering the Allegheny River, where Celeron passed by on his way down the Allegheny River. *Courtesy of Andrew Myers.*

Lake; it then followed the Chadakoin River and Conewango Creek to the Allegheny River, reaching it on July 29, 1749.[257]

In order to mark France's claim to the territories the expedition was passing through, tin or copper plates bearing the French royal arms were nailed to trees. Below, inscribed leaden plates were buried, declaring the claims of France. The plates were buried at Conewango Creek, on the site of the present-day town of Warren. The plates were eleven inches long, seven and a half inches wide, and one-eighth of an inch thick. A translated account of DeCeleron's actions follows:

> *In the year one thousand seven hundred and forty-nine, we, Celeron, knight of the Royal and Military Order of St. Louis, captain commanding a detachment sent by order of the Marquis de la Galissonniere, captain general in Canada, and the beautiful river, otherwise called the Ohio, accompanied by the principal officers of our detachment, have buried at the foot of a red oak tree, on the south bank of the River* Ohio [during their occupation of this region, the French always termed

> the Allegheny River the River Ohio, and this name is also printed on all their early maps] *and opposite the point of a little island, where the two rivers, Ohio and Kanaougou* [from the French standpoint, the name of a Native village] *unite, a leaden plate… with an inscription.*[258]

The inscription recorded the day and year, "twentieth day of July, one thousand seven hundred and forty-nine," the purpose of the expedition, "to re-establish peace in some Indian villages," and ended simply with "Signed by all the officers. Celeron."[259]

Not all of the plates buried by the Celeron expedition have been found, including the plate that was buried in Warren. In the 1940s and 1950s, Merle Deardorff, a Warren banker and amateur historian, investigated Celeron's expedition and the location of all the plates. Deardorff told of O.H. Marshall, the discoverer of Celeron's journal, when he came to Warren to search for the plate buried at the foot of an oak tree at the mouth of Conewango Creek.

Marshall, along with Struthers (a local lawyer) and Cogswell (an old riverman) set out to find the spot Celeron cited in his journal. According to Deardorff, the year was 1882. The old riverman remembered a tree that stood near the bank years before but noted that the river had widened over the years by "20 feet or more," recalling, "A tree approximately opposite the old mouth of the creek…had been undermined in the spring of 1826 or 1827."[260] Struthers also remembered a tree lying in the river at that same point when he came to Warren in 1818. According to Struthers, "It went out the following spring."[261] Apparently, it was washed away by flooding or high waters. Deardorff wrote, "The party concluded that this was the oak mentioned by Celeron and that the plate had gone down the river with it, entangled in its roots."[262]

Part of a Leaden Plate Buried by Celeron de Bienville in Ohio River Valley, 1749. Courtesy of the New York Public Library Digital Collection.

Since 1968, a flag-raising event has been held in Crescent Park in Warren to celebrate the history of the area. Flags representing the four nations that "held sway over the county" are raised as follows: the flag for the Seneca Nation of Natives who first held the land; the French fleur-de-lis, which made claims in the 1600s; the king's colors, representing the British claim; and the American Betsy Ross flag.[263]

General William Irvine

In 1795, a surveying team led by General William Irvine and Andrew Ellicott came to the region and laid out the town of Warren. The first structure was a log building that was erected by the Holland Land Company as a supply depot.

Irvine, born in Enniskillen, Ireland, on November 3, 1741, received a private secondary education and studied medicine in Dublin. He served in the British navy as a ship's surgeon during the French and Indian War. Finding himself in conflict with his commanding officer, he relocated to Carlisle, Pennsylvania, where he established a medical practice in 1764.[264]

A Scottish Ulsterman, Irvine supported the revolutionary movement from the beginning. In 1775, he raised and commanded the Seventh Pennsylvania Regiment as its colonel. Captured at Three Rivers during the American expedition into Canada, he was released in May 1778. Reentering the fight, he was at the Battle of Monmouth (New Jersey), took part in the expedition against Staten Island and served in General Wayne's unsuccessful attack at Bull's Ferry. On George Washington's recommendation, in 1781, the Continental Congress gave Irvine command of the northwest frontier, where he was stationed at Fort Pitt until the end of the war.[265]

In 1785, the commonwealth, anxious for the settlement of "unused" land and to pay its soldiers for their service in the Revolution, created "donation lands" from the Purchase of 1784. The lands were located in Butler, Clarion, Crawford, Erie, Lawrence, Mercer, Venango and Warren Counties. Irvine, with considerable knowledge of the area, was chosen to "survey and dispense these donation lands." Veterans received donations according to their rank and years of service. A private could receive two hundred acres, while a general could receive as much as two thousand.[266]

Irvine recognized the importance of the triangular area near Erie and convinced the commonwealth to buy it, which provided a port for landlocked Pennsylvania. He was responsible for laying out a wide boulevard that extended from Conewango Creek in North Warren to the Allegheny River and down the Allegheny River to the West End. Forty years later, the town council cut the boulevard into town lots and sold them.[267]

General William Irvine. Courtesy of Wikimedia Commons.

With Irvine involved for several years in the surveys as commissioner for the commonwealth, he selected three thousand acres around the mouth of Brokenstraw Creek, apparently for his son, Callender Irvine; it was an estate that was similar to that of his ancestors in Enniskillen, Ireland.

Callender Irvine came to the area in 1795 and erected a cabin. Over a period of time, he became great friends with Chief Cornplanter. In fact, the account says that Cornplanter actually saved Callender Irvine's life. It seems that two Monsey Natives had arrived at Irvine's cabin asking for salt, which was precious in those days. Irvine's servant gave them a little, but they wanted more and vowed they would "have it by fair means or foul." Irvine drove them off the property. In a few days, one of Cornplanter's men came to visit and hunt, spending two weeks with Callender Irvine. Since it was not uncommon for the Natives to stay with him, Callender thought nothing more about it. Months later, Cornplanter told Irvine that the Monseys "had threatened his [Callender Irvine's] life and that he had sent the Indian down secretly to watch their movements."[268]

In 1822, Callender Irvine built a stately white mansion on the banks of the Allegheny River. The village of Irvine was created out of the original land given by General William Irvine. His descendants continued to live in that location, much of it being developed by the son of Callender Irvine, Dr. William Irvine. The National Register of Historic Places has included the stone church, known as the Presbyterian Church at Irvine, that was built by Dr. William Irvine for his wife. General William Irvine's descendants continued to live on portions of the property until the death of Esther Newbold in 1963. The property has become part of the Allegheny National Forest's 513,000-acre forest.

General William Irvine died in July 1804, in Philadelphia, Pennsylvania. His obituary noted that he was "the faithful, virtuous and affectionate husband, the fond and tender parent."[269]

Irvine United Presbyterian Church, National Register of Historic Places, National Park Service. *Courtesy of Wikimedia Commons.*

Passenger Pigeons Fill the Skies

I remember an elderly woman in my hometown of Ridgway who was the granddaughter of early pioneers in the region. She enjoyed talking about the days when the skies over this area of Pennsylvania were filled with passenger pigeons, a species that vanished over the years.

One account by a veteran of the Civil War explains why the passenger pigeon made such an impression on all who witnessed them.

> *You'd think it was thunder rolling when the pigeons came to eat the fallen mast, he said as though he still heard the beat of a million wings. A flock would land then move like a tide, easting acorns. Then another bunch would land ahead of them, and the flocks would leapfrog until they ate every acorn and beechnut on the forest floor. It was like waves breaking and rolling, and it sounded like ten regiments of drummers each time a bunch got up to move ahead of the ones behind it.*[270]

The Seneca Natives relied on passenger pigeons as a food staple. As soon as the Natives completed their annual store of maple sugar early in the spring, it was followed by gathering young passenger pigeons (squabs), just ahead of the time the young ones were ready to leave the nest.

There was more to the hunt for passenger pigeons than merely collecting them as a food staple. The Seneca considered the hunt a religious obligation. Believing that the Creator provided for and sent the pigeons on an annual

Left: *In Visitation, 2004*. A large flock of passenger pigeons gorge themselves in a field strewn with fruit and nuts. *By Walton Ford, Smithsonian American Art Museum.*

Below: *Passenger Pigeon Shoot*, a depiction of a shooting in northern Louisiana by Bennett Smith, 1875. *Courtesy of Wikimedia Commons.*

basis, the Seneca prayed that this blessing from the Creator would always continue. As a matter of fact, the Senecas were conservationists of sorts. While the birds were hatching, the Seneca did not allow hunting for the parent birds over a concern that the newly hatched pigeons would starve if the parents were killed. While the pigeon hunts were intense, there was consideration given to saving some of the parent birds and their young offspring for another year.

Hunting methods among the Seneca varied. According to one eyewitness, in 1850, "nets of bark and twine…were spread for pigeons and quails."[271] While the nets could be dropped on pigeons as they landed on the ground, they could also be used in the trees. Another method was to cut down the roosting trees to gather up thousands of birds. The birds were killed, dressed and suspended on poles in front of fires, where they were dried in the heat and smoke. "When properly cured, they were packed in bags or baskets for transportation to the home towns. It was a festival season…and even the meanest dog in camp had his fill of pigeon meat."[272] When the birds arrived in swarms, the Natives hunted them by gun, "using a single discharge of bird-shot, they could sometimes kill as many as 50 or more."[273]

According to the Pennsylvania Game Commission, passenger pigeons nested in large colonies in Cameron, Elk, Forest, McKean, Potter and Warren Counties. "Substantial rookeries, or 'cities,' as some called them, were reportedly located near Kane, Oil City, Pigeon, Sheffield and Brookston, and Conneaut and Pymatuning Marshes."[274] Nesting areas could be up to two miles wide, with so many birds nesting in the trees that tree limbs would break.

Through the early years of settlement in the Pennsylvania Wilds region, the residents followed the Native tradition of hunting the pigeons, taking what they needed and nothing more. In the later 1800s, however, the demand for pigeons increased. In a 1931 newspaper interview with the *Warren Times Mirror*, eighty-two-year-old Edward T. Barnes of Barnes (Warren County, Pennsylvania) recalled his experiences in hunting passenger pigeons.

> *In 1870, I lived with my parents in Saybrook, about one and one-half miles north of Sheffield on the Warren and Ridgway Turnpike, and began my work catching pigeons….A salt bed which had been set with a net about sixteen by thirty-five feet spread over it. The operator being concealed in a bough house from which the net was sprung…The catch running around fifty dozen.*

Martha, the Last Passenger Pigeon. Photograph by Donald E. Hurlbert, Smithsonian Institution.

It was the growing demand for pigeons that eventually led to the demise of the species. Professional hunters began to enter the pigeon nesting areas, taking huge numbers of birds, with devastating results. As recorded by one historian, "The American Express Company carried, in one day, over the New York and Erie Railroad, over seven tons of pigeons to the New York market, and all of these were from the west of Corning, [New York].[275] The Pennsylvania Game Commission, recalling the vast numbers of passenger pigeons in north America, recorded that, in 1859, in the town of Hartford, Michigan, "three railcar loads of passenger pigeons were shipped to market daily for forty days. The carcasses totaled more than eleven million over that period."[276] Mr. Barnes, who was quoted earlier in a newspaper interview, also remembered seeing flocks of birds that were over a mile wide and would take two hours to pass over.

In the time of the Seneca Native hunts for passenger pigeons, no one missed the annual fun. An important part of their culture and religion, it was said that marriages were contracted at the pigeon hunts, as it was a time when the Natives could assemble and work together.[277]

The last passenger pigeon, Martha, who lived at the Cincinnati Zoo, died in 1914 and is preserved at the Smithsonian Institute. As one Civil War veteran observed, "The woods were silent now. They had been silent during the years I had grown to manhood."[278]

29.
CONCLUSION

What started out as a genealogical journey back in time to learn more about one of my family lines that came to the Pennsylvania Wilds seven generations ago developed into a wider story of the events that led up to the settlement of this region and the events that shaped the lives of those early people.

The story of the Wilds is the story of migration. Through the study of DNA, we know that, thousands of years ago, Indians who were located in Asia migrated east to the "New World," continually expanding eastward until those tribes familiar to us in recent history were residing in the eastern United States. Europeans were also comprised of groups of tribes trekking westward across Europe for thousands of years, settling in various regions that eventually became the modern countries we recognize today. Citizens of those countries continued a westward migration and began arriving in the New World in the 1600s. Eastward-bound people met westward-bound people, and they became what is referred to as the "melting pot" of the world.

One phrase has continually gone through my mind as I have researched this book. "Man's inhumanity to man," credited to Scottish poet Bobby Burns. In our account about the Natives and Colonials, both sides traded in "man's inhumanity to man"; it is almost incomprehensible cruelty to the minds of twenty-first-century Americans. As such, I believe we must reflect on the points of view on each side of the conflict, not just one side.

Two "Wilds" Boys Looking Out over the Forest in a Rock Shelter Once Used by the Indians. Courtesy of Andrew Myers.

I ask, "What if?" What if the two greatest powers on earth at the time, the French and British, had not had different objectives in the settlement of the New World? What if the British had been more sympathetic to the Natives' hopes of keeping lands in the Ohio Valley? If not for Braddock's "that no savage should inherit the land" statement, they may have sided with the British during the French and Indian War rather than allying with the French. What if Chief White Eyes, the Native chief who was offered a separate fourteenth state by the Continental government, had not died? Would he have accepted the offer and allied his people with the Continental government, making relations between the settlers and the Natives significantly different? Would the lands in the Last Purchase of 1784, which encompasses the region of the Pennsylvania Wilds, have been designated as a separate Native state?

At one point in the book, I noted that, following the French and Indian War, the colonials realized they could take on the most powerful force in the world at that time, Great Britain, and defeat them in the American Revolution. James Smith, a famous White Indian, addressed that fact in his writings forty years after he was taken captive. In his own words, Smith reflected on the art of Indian war learned by the settlers that was useful in fighting the Revolution:

> *Is it not the best discipline that has the greatest tendency to annoy the enemy and save their own men? I apprehend that the Indian discipline is as well calculated to answer the purpose of the woods of America, as the British discipline in Flanders; and British discipline in the woods, is the way to have men slaughtered with scarcely any chance of defending themselves.*[279]
>
> *Let us take a view of the benefits we have received, by what little we have learned of their* [Indian's] *art of war, which cost us dear, and the loss that we have sustained for want of it, and then see if it will not be well worth our while to retain what we have, and also to endeavor to improve in this necessary branch of business. Though we have made considerable proficient in this line, and in some respects out-do them, viz. as marksmen, and in cutting our rifles, and in keeping them in good order; yet, I append we are far behind in their maneuvers, or in being able to surprise, or prevent a surprise. May we not conclude that the progress we had made in their art of war, contributed considerably towards our success, in various respects, when contending with Great Britain for liberty? Had the British King attempted to enslave us before Braddock's war* [French and Indian War], *in all probability, he might readily have done it, because, except the New-Englanders, who had formerly been engaged in war, with the Indians, we were unacquainted with any kind of war: but after fighting such a subtle and barbarous enemy as the Indians, we were not terrified at the approach of British red-coats.*[280]

While the Delaware Tribe was found throughout Pennsylvania in those early years, in the end, they were driven out. Shingas's followers went to Canada, where there is still a small community in Brantford, Ontario. A larger group of Delaware resides in Oklahoma.[281] For those interested in translations of Delaware Native names that are familiar to Pennsylvanians, search the Lenape Talking Dictionary at www.talk-lenape.org.

Here, I have presented brief vignettes of early settlers in the Pennsylvania Wilds. You will recognize that they were Patriots of the Revolution—or children of the Patriots—who lived through those trying times. Because of their experiences, they were strong, self-sufficient people who laid the ground work for the communities where we reside today. Many who live here are the direct descendants of those early people.

Following the original settlers, who were, for the most part, of English, Irish, Scotch-Irish and German extraction, waves of others migrated into the region, looking for their place in the great melting pot of the United States. Timbering, coal mining and manufacturing led to the need for people to fill jobs in those industries. Their varied ethnic backgrounds have also been an influence on the transformation of the Wilds. But that is a story for another time.

Notes

Introduction

1. Pennsylvania Wilds, "About."
2. Ibid.
3. Donehoo, *Indian Villages and Place*, various pages.

Chapter 1

4. *McKean, Elk, and Forest*, 95.
5. Donehoo, *Indian Villages and Place*, 2.
6. Ibid., 5.
7. Wallace, *Indian Paths*, map, "Key to the Indian Paths of Pennsylvania," (no page number assigned).

Chapter 2

8. Ibid., back cover.
9. Ibid., 1–2.
10. Ibid., 68.
11. Jordan, "Ettwein's Notes," 208–19.
12. Wallace, *Indian Paths*, 71.
13. Ibid., 10.
14. Ibid., 6.

Chapter 3

15. Pennsylvania Historical and Museum Commission, "Quaker Province."
16. Thursday advertisements, *Pennsylvania Gazette*, 4.
17. Ibid.
18. Pennsylvania Historical and Museum Commission, "Quaker Province."
19. Donehoo, *Indian Villages and Place*, 16.
20. Wallace, *Conrad Weiser*, 294–97.
21. Ibid.
22. Ibid.

Chapter 4

23. "Dinwiddie's Letter," *Pennsylvania Gazette*, 1.
24. Ibid.

Chapter 5

25. Steele, *Captives Free*, 395.
26. "Defeat," *Pennsylvania Gazette*, 2.

Chapter 6

27. Long, *Lord Jeffrey Amherst*, 186.

Chapter 7

28. Wallace, *Indians*, 3.
29. Ibid., 7.
30. Ibid., 50.
31. Newcomb, *Culture and Acculturation*, 55.
32. Harrington, *Religion and Ceremonies*, 23.
33. Wallace, *Indians*, 75.
34. Collier, *Indians of the Americas*, 214–15.
35. Wallace, *Indians*, 70, 71.
36. Ibid., 79.

37. Ibid., 179.
38. Ibid.
39. Myers, *Narrative*, 230, 232–33.
40. Wallace, *Indians*, 19.
41. Ibid., 21.
42. Ibid., 20.
43. Ibid., 30, 31.

Chapter 8

44. LeRoy, "John Jacob LeRoy," 6.
45. LeRoy and Leininger, *Narrative*, 407.
46. Ibid.
47. Ibid.
48. "Attack," *Pennsylvania Gazette*, 2.

Chapter 9

49. Wallace, *Indians*, 21, 22, 47.
50. Ibid., 47.
51. Fleming, *William and Elizabeth Fleming*, 3.
52. Ibid.
53. Ibid., 5.
54. Ibid., 6–7.
55. Ibid., 10.
56. Bond, "Captivity," 63–64.
57. Fleming, *William and Elizabeth Fleming*, 14.
58. Ward, "Redeeming," 167.

Chapter 10

59. Ibid., 165.
60. Wallace, *Indians*, 48.
61. DiAngelis, "Determining Reliability in Indian Captivity Narratives," master's thesis, College of William and Mary, Arts and Sciences, 2010, www.scholarworks.wm.edu.
62. Steele, *Captives Free*, 218–19.

Chapter 11

63. Sever, *Mary Jemison*, 27–28.

Chapter 12

64. Donehoo, *Indian Villages and Place*, 164.
65. Ibid.
66. Wallace, *Indian Paths*, 68.
67. Jordan, "Ettwein's Notes," 208–19.
68. Donehoo, *Indian Villages and Place*, 163.
69. Ibid., 163.
70. Ibid., 164.
71. Steele, *Captives Free*, 373.
72. "Another Attack," *Pennsylvania Gazette*, 2.
73. LeRoy and Leininger, *Narrative*, 410.
74. Ibid., 411.
75. Steele, *Captives Free*, 244–45.
76. LeRoy, "John Jacob LeRoy," 6.
77. Ibid.
78. Hembree, "Barbara Leininger Comes Home," www.miller-malcolm-familytree.net.

Chapter 13

79. Lambert, "Stockholm Syndrome."
80. J. Smith, *Col. James Smith*, 6, 7, 8, 9, 10, 11.
81. Adlum, *Cultivation of the Vine.*
82. Steele, *Captives Free*, 380.
83. Ibid., 222.
84. Ibid.
85. Ibid., 223.

Chapter 14

86. Stevens and Kent, *Col. Henry Bouquet*, 153.

87. Centers for Disease Control and Prevention, "Smallpox?"
88. Rung, *Chronicles*, 142.
89. Ibid., 142.
90. From the modern dictionary: "A deceitful and unreliable scoundrel; as a synonym: rogue, scoundrel, scamp, villain, miscreant, renegade."
91. Rung, *Chronicles*, 142.
92. Ibid.
93. Ibid., 142–43.
94. Ibid., 143.
95. Ibid.
96. Parkman, *Pontiac, II*, 39.
97. Volwiler, "Trent's Journal," 400.
98. Stevens and Kent, "Levy, Trent and Company: Account against the Crown, Aug. 13, 1763," in *Col. Henry Bouquet.*
99. Fenn, "Biological Warfare."
100. Rung, *Chronicles*, 142.
101. "Bouquet's March," *Pennsylvania Gazette*, 3.

Chapter 15

102. Ibid., 2.
103. Ward, "Redeeming," 188.
104. Steele, *Captives Free*, 338.
105. Ibid.
106. "Empowering Life," *Intelligencer: Wheeling News-Register*, 1–3.
107. "Recovered," *Pennsylvania Gazette*, 3.
108. Steele, *Captives Free*, 335.

Chapter 16

109. Rowe, "Frederick Stump Affair," 260–61.
110. Minutes of the Provincial Council of Pennsylvania, vol. 9, "Murdered Indians at Stump Creek," Philadelphia, Pennsylvania, January 16, 1768, and February 17, 1768.
111. Ibid.

Chapter 17

112. Wallace, *Indians*, 159–60.

Chapter 18

113. Ibid., 160–61.
114. Ibid., 160.

Chapter 19

115. Bakeless, *Turncoats*, 296, 297.
116. Donehoo, *Indian Villages and Place*, 23, 24.
117. Founders Online, "To George Washington from William Patterson, 3 April 1779," www.founders.archives.gov.
118. Bakeless, *Turncoats*, 297.
119. Ibid., 297.
120. Ibid., 297–98.
121. Ibid., 298.

Chapter 20

122. Meginness, *Journal*, 30.
123. Ibid., 30.
124. Ibid., 34.
125. Ibid., 33.
126. Ibid., 61.
127. Ibid, 61, 62, 63.

Chapter 21

128. Pennsylvania Historical and Museum Commission, "RG-17."
129. Hermansen, "Boundary Retracement Principles and Procedures for Pennsylvania, 3.1.2, Boundary Retracement, Records of the Land Office 3," Pennsylvania Society of Land Surveyors, 2004.

130. Black, Ruffner and Abrams, "Native American Influences," 1,266–76.
131. Love, "Chapter 1: Introduction," 1.
132. Knud Everett Hermansen, "7.2.1. Locative, Passing and Witness."
133. Wikipedia, "Holland Land Company," www.wikipedia.com.
134. "75,000 Acres of Land," *Lancaster Intelligencer*, March 14, 1809, 4.
135. "118 Tracts of Lands," *Lancaster Intelligencer*, February 4, 1813, 6.
136. Kane Area Development Center, "History."
137. Casler, *Tionesta*, 802.

Chapter 22

138. "Season," *United States Gazette*, 1.
139. "Summerless Year," *Jeffersonian Democrat*, 1.
140. Bellville, "Year Without."
141. Wikipedia, "Year Without a Summer," www.wikipedia.com.
142. McKnight, *Pioneer History*, 227, 228.

Chapter 23

143. Pennsylvania Great Outdoors Visitors Bureau, "Discover."
144. Donehoo, *Indian Villages and Place*, 206.
145. Ibid.
146. Meginness, *Journal*, 29.
147. Donehoo, *Indian Villages and Place*, 206.
148. *History of the Counties*, 823.
149. Wallace, *Paths*, 126.
150. Jones, *Juniata Valley*, 253.
151. *History of the Counties*, 825, 826.
152. Cox, "Transition."
153. Donehoo, *Indian Villages and Place*, 206.
154. *History of the Counties*, 823.
155. Union County Historical Society, "Catherine Smith."
156. *History of the Counties*, 834–35.

Chapter 24

157. Clearfield County, Pennsylvania, "Homepage."
158. Caldwell, *Atlas of Clearfield County*, 10.
159. Aldrich, *Clearfield County*, 472.
160. Futhey and Cope, *Chester County*, 772.
161. Ancestry, "Tax Records, 1786 New London, Chester, PA," www.ancestry.com; Ancestry, "Tax Records, 1787 Chester County Tax District," www.ancestry.com.
162. Aldrich, *Clearfield County*, 475.
163. Ibid., 474–75.
164. Donehoo, *Indian Villages and Place*, 28.
165. Aldrich, *Clearfield County*, 280, 281.
166. McKnight and Brookville, *Pioneer Outline*, 156.
167. "King Hunter," *Progress*, 6.
168. Ibid.
169. Aldrich, *Clearfield County*, 280.
170. "School," *Clearfield Republican*, 1.
171. "Qualifications," *Progress*, 18.

Chapter 25

172. Pennsylvania Historical and Museum Commission, "Clinton County."
173. Wallace, *Indians*, 8.
174. Ibid., 61.
175. Maynard, *Historical View*, 134.
176. Meginness, *History*, 1.
177. Ibid, 2.
178. Donehoo, *Indian Villages and Place*, 12.
179. Clinton County Genealogical Society, "Great Island."
180. Ibid.
181. Ibid.
182. "Penn Visited," *Express*, 7.
183. Ibid.
184. Ibid.
185. Woulfe, "Irish Names."
186. Linn, *Centre and Clinton Counties*, 471.
187. Ibid., 15.

188. Ibid., 22.
189. Ancestry, "Kelly Family Tree."
190. Editors of Encyclopaedia Britannica, "Lock Haven."
191. Bernard, "Jerry Church."
192. Ibid.
193. Editors of Encyclopaedia Britannica, "Lock Haven."

Chapter 26

194. *McKean, Elk, and Forest*, 589.
195. Ibid.
196. Ibid.
197. Fagan, "Elk or Wapiti."
198. Kosack, "Pennsylvania Elk."
199. Meginness, *History*, 30.
200. Shea, "Eastern Elk."
201. Stalling, "Eastern Elk."
202. Kosack, "Pennsylvania Elk."
203. "Elk Are Dying," *Harrisburg Daily Independent* (Harrisburg, PA), April 21, 1913, 6.
204. Kosack, "Pennsylvania Elk."
205. Ibid.
206. "Elk Management," *Progress*, 19.
207. Elk Country Visitor Center, "History."
208. Wessman, *History of Elk County*, 280.
209. Ibid., 280.
210. "Pioneer Days," *Courier-Express*, 10.
211. Ibid.
212. *McKean, Elk, and Forest*, 580.
213. Wessman, *History of Elk County*, 303–4.

Chapter 27

214. Jefferson County, Pennsylvania, www.jeffersoncountypa.com.
215. Caldwell, *Atlas of Jefferson County*, 13.
216. Scott, *Jefferson County*, 61–2.
217. McKnight and Brookville, *Her Pioneers and People*, 1.

218. Ibid., 1.
219. Caldwell, *Atlas of Jefferson County*, 13.
220. Ibid.
221. Scott, *Jefferson County*, 35.
222. Ibid., 34.
223. McKnight and Brookville, *Her Pioneers and People*, 1.
224. Scott, *Jefferson County*, 35.
225. Ibid., 36.
226. Ibid., 43.
227. Ibid., 45.
228. Ibid., 37.
229. Ibid., 37.
230. Ibid., 37.
231. Ibid., 38.
232. Caldwell, *Atlas of Jefferson County*, 22.
233. Holton and Holton, *Winslow Memorial, 1888*, 992.
234. Ibid., 233.
235. U.S. Government, "Fourth Amendment to the Constitution," www.constitution.congress.gov.
236. Holton and Holton, *Winslow Memorial, 1888*, 233.
237. "Winslow Family Reunion," *Ridgway Record*, 5.
238. Caldwell, *Jefferson County*, 22.
239. Holton and Holton, *Winslow Memorial, 1888*, 1,003.

Chapter 28

240. McKnight and Brookville, *Pioneer Outline*, 53.
241. Ibid., 54.
242. Wallace, *Indians*, 166.
243. Donehoo, *Indian Villages and Place*, 24.
244. Wallace, *Indians*, 163.
245. Puckett, "History of Corn."
246. "Corn," in *Funk & Wagnalls*.
247. Gibson and Benson, "Origin."
248. Puckett, "History of Corn."
249. Ontario Corn, "History," www.ontariocorn.org.
250. Canfield, *Iroquois*, 51–53.
251. McKnight and Brookville, *Pioneer Outline*, 54.

252. Ibid.
253. Bartlett, "Cornplanter," 1–3.
254. "Flood," *Warren Times Mirror*, 1.
255. B. Smith, "St. Patrick's Day Flood."
256. Burton, "Detroit's Rulers," 328.
257. Schenck and Rann, *Warren County*, 61–62.
258. Ibid, 61.
259. Ibid., 62.
260. Ibid.
261. Ibid.
262. Ibid.
263. Ferry, "4 Flags," 1–5.
264. Pennsylvania Historic and Museum Commission, "William Irvine."
265. Ibid.
266. Ibid.
267. "General William Irvine Chapter," *Warren Tribune*, 5.
268. McKnight and Brookville, *Pioneer Outline*, 649.
269. "Irvine," *Aurora General Advertiser*, 2.
270. Dvorak, "River of Sky."
271. Fenton and Deardorff, "Ethnology," 290.
272. Ibid., 291.
273. Ibid., 290.
274. Pennsylvania Game Commission, "Passenger Pigeon."
275. McKnight and Brookville, *Pioneer Outline*, 159.
276. Pennsylvania Game Commission, www.pgc.pa.gov.
277. Fenton and Deardorff, "Ethnology," 291.
278. Dvorak, "River of Sky."

Chapter 29

279. J. Smith, *Col. James Smith*, 155.
280. Ibid., 156.
281. Wallace, *Indians*, 169.

Bibliography

Abler, Thomas S. *Cornplanter: Chief Warrior of the Allegheny Senecas*. Syracuse, NY: Syracuse University Press, 2007.

Adlum, John A. *A Memoir on the Cultivation of the Vine in America*. Washington, D.C.: Davis and Force, 1823.

Aldrich, Lewis Cass. *History of Clearfield County Pennsylvania*. Syracuse, NY: D. Mason & Co., 1887.

"American Indians." In *Funk & Wagnalls New Encyclopedia*. Vol. 2. Oxford: Oxford University Press, 1993.

Ancestry. "Kelly Family Tree." www.ancestry.com.

Anderson, Fred. *Crucible of War: The Seven Years War and the Fate of the British Empire in North America, 1754–1766*. New York: Alfred A. Knopf, a division of Random House Inc., 2000.

Aurora General Advertiser. "Died—On Sunday evening, of Cholera Morbus, Major General William Irvine." July 31, 1804.

Bakeless, John. *Turncoats, Traitors and Heroes*. Philadelphia: J.B. Lippincott Company, 1959.

Bartlett, Charles E. "Jesse Cornplanter." *New York State Archaeological Association's Bulletin*, no. 10 (July 10, 1957): 1–3.

Bellville, Peter K. "A Year Without a Summer." Church of Jesus Christ of Latter-day Saints, January 1983. www.churchofjesuschrist.org.

Bernard, Lou. "Jerry Church and the City of Mysteries." *Express*, November 2, 2013. www.lockhaven.com.

Black, B.A., C.N. Ruffner and M.D. Abrams. "Native American Influences on the Forest Composition of the Allegheny Plateau, Northwest Pennsylvania." *Canadian Journal of Forest Research* 36, no. 5 (2006): 1,266–76.

Bond, Beverly W., Jr. "The Captivity of Charles Stuart, 1755–1757." *Mississippi Valley Historical Review* 13, no. 1 (1926): 75–80.

Burton, C.M. "Detroit's Rulers." In *Historical Collections of the Michigan Pioneer and Historical Society*. Vol. 34. New York: Wynkoop Hallenbeck Crawford Co., 1905.

Caldwell, J.A. *Illustrated Historical Combination Atlas of Clearfield County, Pennsylvania*. Condit, OH: J.A. Caldwell, 1878.

Canfield, William W. *The Legends of the Iroquois: Told by "The Cornplanter."* New York: Wessels Company, 1902.

Casler, Walter C. *Tionesta Valley*. Logging Railroad Era of Lumbering in Pennsylvania 8. Williamsport, PA: Lycoming Printing Co. Inc., 1977.

Centers for Disease Control and Prevention. "What is Smallpox?" www.CDC.gov.

Clearfield County, Pennsylvania. "Homepage." www.visitclearfieldcounty.org.

Clearfield Republican. "First School." July 23, 1879.

Clinton County Genealogical Society. "Great Island." www.clintoncogensociety.org.

Collier, John. *The Indians of the Americas*. New York: Mentor Books, 1947.

Cook, Frederick. *Journals of the Military Expedition of Major General John Sullivan Against the Six Nations of Indians in 1779*. Auburn, NY: Knapp, Peck & Thompson Printers, 1887.

"Corn." In *Funk & Wagnalls New Encyclopedia*. Vol. 7. Oxford: Oxford University Press, 1993.

Courier-Express. "Pioneer Days in Brady Township." August 10, 1929.

Cox, Thomas R. "Transition in the Woods; Log Drivers, Raftsmen, and the Emergence of Modern Lumbering in Pennsylvania." San Diego State University. www.journals.plu.edu.

DiAngelis, Heather Nicole. "Determining Reliability in Indian Captivity Narratives, 1754–1763." Master's thesis, University of Akron, to the Graduate Faculty of the College of William and Mary, 2010. www.scholarworks.wm.edu.

Dixon, Cyril W. *Smallpox*. London: J. and A. Churchill Ltd., 1963.

Donehoo, Dr. George P. *A History of the Indian Villages and Place Names in Pennsylvania*. Reprint, Lewisburg, PA: Wennawoods Publishing, 2010.

Dvorak, Ed, Jr. "River of Sky." Project Passenger Pigeon. www.passengerpigeon.org.

Editors of Encyclopaedia Britannica. "The History of Corn." www.britannica.com.

———. "Lock Haven." www.britannica.com.

Elk Country Visitor Center. "History: (Re)Introducing the Elk." www.elkcountryvisitorcenter.com.

Explore PA History. "Irvine." www.explorepahistory.com

Express. "It May Be Myth, but Legend Has It Penn Visited on Great Island Here." June 28, 1951.

Fagan, Damian. "Elk or Wapiti. Cervus elaphas—Elk, Deer, and Moose Family—Cervidae." DesertUSA. www.desertusa.com.

Fenn, Elizabeth A. "Biological Warfare in Eighteenth Century North America: Beyond Jeffrey Amherst." *Journal of American History* 86, no. 4 (2000): 1,553–558.

Fenton, William N., and Merle H. Deardorff. "Ethnology: The Last Passenger Pigeon Hunts of the Cornplanter Senecas." *Journal of the Washington Academy of Sciences* 33, no. 10 (October 15, 1943): 289–315.

Ferry, Brian. "4 Flags Unfurled to Celebrate our History." *Warren Times Observer*, May 27, 2019.

Fleming, William. *A Narrative of the Sufferings and Surprising Deliverances of William and Elizabeth Fleming*. Boston: Green & Russell, 1778. www.founders.archives.gov.

Frantz, John B., and William Pencak. *Beyond Philadelphia: The American Revolution in the Pennsylvania Hinterland*. University Park: Penn State University Press, 1998.

"French and Indian War." In *Funk & Wagnalls New Encyclopedia*. Vol. 10. Oxford: Oxford University Press, 1993.

Futhey, J. Smith, and Gilbert Cope. *History of Chester County, Pennsylvania*. Philadelphia: Louis H. Everts, 1881.

Gibson, Lance, and Garren Benson. "Origin, History and Uses of Corn (Zea mays)." Iowa State University, Department of Agronomy. www.scrip.org.

Greathead, Elsie S. *The History of Fulton County, Pennsylvania*. Created 1936. McConnellsburg, PA: *Fulton County News*, n.d.

Hamel, Elsie. "The Walking Purchase Fraud of 1737." Essay, Lehigh University, December 12, 2014, www.digital.lib.lehigh.edu.

Harrington, M.R. *Religion and Ceremonies of the Lenape*. New York: Museum of the American Indian, Heye Foundation, 1921.

Hermansen, Knud Everett, PhD, PLS, PE, Esq. "Boundary Retracement Principles and Procedures for Pennsylvania, 3.1.2, Boundary Retracement, Records of the Land Office 3." Pennsylvania Society of Land Surveyors, 2004.

History of Bedford, Somerset and Fulton Counties. Chicago: Waterman, Watkins & Company, 1884.

History of the Counties of McKean, Elk, Cameron and Potter, Pennsylvania. Chicago: J.H. Beers & Co., 1890.

Holton, David Parsons, AM, MD, and Frances K. Holton. *Winslow Memorial, 1888*. New York: D.P. Holton, 1888

Intelligencer: Wheeling News-Register. "Some Captives Chose Native Americans' Empowering Life." June 26, 2016. www.theintelligencer.net.

Jefferson County, Pennsylvania. www.jeffersoncountypa.com.

Jeffersonian Democrat. "The Summerless Year." April 10, 1878.

Jones, U.J. *History of the Settlement of the Juniata Valley*. Philadelphia: Henry B. Ashmend, 1856.

Jordan, John W. *A History of the Juniata Valley and its People*. Vol. 2. New York: Lewis Historical Publishing Company, 1913.

———. "Rev. John Ettwein's Notes of Travel from the North Branch of the Susquehanna to the Beaver River, Pennsylvania, 1772." *Pennsylvania Magazine of History and Biography* 25 (1901): 208–19.

Kane Area Development Center. "History of Kane." www.Kanepa.com.

Kirby, C.D. *The Early History of the Cattaraugus, Gowanda, NY*. Grand Island, NY: Niagara Frontier Publishing Co. Inc./Gowanda Bicentennial Committee Inc., 1976.

Klingaman, William K., and Nicholas P. Klingaman. *Year Without a Summer: 1816 and the Volcano That Darkened the World and Changed History*. New York: St. Martin's Press, 2013.

Kosack, Joe, wildlife education specialist. "History of Pennsylvania Elk." Pennsylvania Game Commission. www.pgc.pa.gov.

Lambert, Laura. "Stockholm Syndrome." www.britannica.com.

LeRoy, Marie. "John Jacob LeRoy." *Altoona Tribune*, June 13, 1949.

LeRoy, Marie and Barbara Leininger. *The Narrative of Marie LeRoy and Barbara Leininger, for Three Years Captives Among the Indians*. Translated by Right Reverend Edmund de Schweirnitz, Bethlehem, with a few annotations by the editor of *Penna Magazine*. Philadelphia, PA: Pamphlet in the Library of the Historical Society of Pennsylvania, 1759.

Linn, John Blair. *History of Centre and Clinton Counties, Pennsylvania*. Philadelphia, PA: Louis H. Everts, 1883.

Long, J.C. *Lord Jeffrey Amherst: A Soldier of the King*. New York: Macmillan Publishers, 1933.

Love, J. Barry, PhD. "The Colonial Surveyor in Pennsylvania." *Pennsylvania Society of Land Surveyors*, 2000, 1.

Maynard, D.S. *Historical View of Clinton County, from Its Earliest Settlement to the Present Time*. Lock Haven, PA: Enterprise Printing House, 1875.

McKnight, W.J. *A Pioneer History of Jefferson County, Pennsylvania*. Philadelphia: J.B. Lippencott Company, 1898.

McKnight, W.J. and M.D. Brookville. *Jefferson County, Pennsylvania: Her Pioneers and People*. Chicago: J.H. Beers and Co., 1917.

———. *A Pioneer Outline History of Northwestern Pennsylvania*. Philadelphia: J.B. Lippencott Co., 1905.

Meginness, John F. *History of the Great Island and William Dunn, Its Owner, and Founder of Dunnstown*. Williamsport, PA: Gazette and Bulletin Printing House, 1894.

———. *Journal of Samuel Maclay, While Surveying the West Branch of the Susquehanna, the Sinnemahoning, and the Allegheny Rivers in 1790*. Williamsport, PA: Gazette and Bulletin Printing House, 1887.

Miner, Charles. *History of Wyoming, in a Series of Letters from Charles Miner to His Son, William Penn Miner, Esq*. Philadelphia: J. Crissy, 1845.

Minutes of the Provincial Council of Pennsylvania. Vol. 9. "Murdered Indians at Stump Creek." Philadelphia, Pennsylvania, January 16, 1768, and February 17, 1768.

Myers, Albert Cook, ed. *Narrative of Early Pennsylvania, West New Jersey, and Delaware, 1640–1707*. New York: Charles Scribner's Sons, 1912.

Newcomb, William W., Jr. *The Culture and Acculturation of the Delaware Indians*. Ann Arbor: University of Michigan, 1956.

Parkman, Frances. *Conspiracy of Pontiac, II*. Boston: C.C. Little & J. Brown, 1851.

Pennsylvania Game Commission. "Passenger Pigeon: Species Profile." www.pgc.pa.gov.

Pennsylvania Gazette. "Another Attack on Great Cove." January 18, 1756.

———. "Attack at Penn's Creek." October 30, 1755.

———. "Bouquet's March on the Ohio." September 27, 1764.

———. "Braddock's Defeat." July 31, 1755.

———. "Copy of Governor Dinwiddie's Letter to the Commandant of the French Forces on the Ohio, Sent by Major Washington and Reply." March 26, 1754.

———. "Notice Captives Recovered." February 21, 1765.

———. Thursday advertisements. October 30, 1755.

Pennsylvania Great Outdoors Visitors Bureau. "Discover Cameron County." www.visitpago.com.

Pennsylvania Historical and Museum Commission. "Clinton County." www.phmc.pa.gov.

———. "General William Irvine Donation Lands Historic Marker." www.explorepahistory.com.

———. "RG-17, Records of the Land Office." www.phmc.state.pa.us.

———. "1681–1776: The Quaker Province, the Founding of Pennsylvania." www.phmc.state.pa.us.

———. "The Walking Purchase, PHMC, Our Document Heritage." www.phmc.state.pa.us.

Pennsylvania Wilds. "About the Pennsylvania Wilds." www.pawilds.com.

Pittsburgh History 75, no. 1 (Spring 1992). www.journals.psu.ed.

Progress. "Elk Management Area Proposed." November 20, 1970.

———. "King Hunter of Pennsylvania." November 17, 1951.

———. "Schoolmaster's Qualifications." July 13, 1974.

Puckett, Kori. "The History of Corn: Corn History in American Cuisine." RLRouse Directory of Informational Resources. www.rlrouse.com.

Ridgway Record. "Report of the Winslow Family Reunion of August 29, 1908." September 2, 1908.

Ronlet, Philip. "The British, the Indians, and Smallpox: What Actually Happened at Fort Pitt in 1763?" Hunter College. www.journals.psu.edu.

Rowe, G.S. "The Frederick Stump Affair, 1768, and Its Challenge to Loyal Historians of Early Pennsylvania." University of Northern Colorado. www.journals.psu.edu.

Rung, Albert M. *Rung's Chronicles of Pennsylvania History.* Vol. 2. Huntingdon, PA: Huntingdon County Historical Society, 1951–57.

Schenk, J.S. *History of Warren County, Pennsylvania.* Syracuse, NY: D. Mason & Company, 1887.

Schenck, J.S., and W.S. Rann. *History of Warren County, Pennsylvania.* Syracuse, NY: D. Mason & Co., 1887.

Scott, Kate M. *History of Jefferson County, PA.* Syracuse, NY: D. Mason & Co., 1888.

Sever, Robert E. *A Narrative of the Life of Mrs. Mary Jemison.* Canandaigua, NY: J.D. Bemis & Company, 1824.

Shea, Susan. "Remembering the Eastern Elk." January 14, 2019. www.northernwoodlands.org.

Shoemaker, Henry W. *Juniata Memories.* Philadelphia: John Joseph McVey, 1830.

Sipe, C. Hale. "The Indian Wars of Pennsylvania." *Telegraph Press,* 1929.

Smith, Brady. "The St. Patrick's Day Flood of 1936." Senator John Heinz History Center, March 16, 2017. www.heinzhistorycenter.org.

Smith, James. *An Account of the Remarkable Occurrences in the Life and Travels of Col. James Smith.* Lexington, KY: John Bradford, 1797.

Stalling, David. "Eastern Elk: Are They Really Extinct." *Bugle*, Spring 1994. www.ostego.org.

Steele, Ian K. *Setting All the Captives Free, Capture, Adjustment and Recollection in Allegheny Country*. Montreal, CA: McGill-Queen's University Press, 2013.

Stevens, Sylvester K., and Donald H. Kent, eds. *The Papers of Col. Henry Bouquet*. Harrisburg: Department of Public Instruction, Pennsylvania Historical Commission, 1940–1943.

Union County Historical Society. "The Remarkable Widow Catherine Smith." www.unioncountyhistoricalsociety.org

United States Gazette. "The Season." July 31, 1816.

Volwiler, A.T. "William Trent's Journal at Fort Pitt, 1763." *Mississippi Valley Historical Review* 11, no. 3 (December 1924): 390–413.

Wallace, Paul A.W. *Conrad Weiser, 1696–1760; Friend of Colonist and Mohawk*. Philadelphia: University of Pennsylvania Press, 1945.

———. *Indians in Pennsylvania*. Harrisburg: Commonwealth of Pennsylvania, Pennsylvania Historical and Museum Commission, 1964.

———. *Indian Paths of Pennsylvania*. Harrisburg: Commonwealth of Pennsylvania, Pennsylvania Historical and Museum Commission, 2005.

Ward, Matthew C. "Redeeming the Captives: Pennsylvania Captives Among the Ohio Indians, 1755–1765." *Pennsylvania Magazine of History and Biography* 125, no. 3 (July 2001): 161–89.

Warren Times Mirror. "Flood Menace Returns." March 17, 1936.

Warren Tribune. "Report of the Organization of the General William Irvine Chapter, National Society, Daughters of 1812." November 3, 1926.

Weislager, C.A. *The Delaware Indians*. New Brunswick, NJ: Rutgers University Press, 1972.

Wessman, Alice L., principal author, historian, editor and compiler. *A History of Elk County, Pennsylvania*. Ridgway, PA: Elk County Historical Society, 1981.

Woulfe, Reverend Patrick. "Irish Names and Surnames." 1923. www.libraryireland.com.

About the Author

Kathy Myers is a native of Ridgway, Elk County, Pennsylvania, where she has spent most of her life. She was the director of marketing at Elk County General Hospital in Ridgway, and prior to her retirement, she was the owner of Area Abstracting and Filing Service, a real estate settlement/title abstract company serving attorneys in Clearfield and Jefferson Counties.

A member of the seventh generation of her family to live in the Wilds, Myers is a historian, genealogist and writer who now resides in the Beechwoods of Jefferson County. She is a member of the General Society of Mayflower Descendants (GSMD), the governor of the Winslow Heritage Society, a member of the DuBois Area Historical Society and a member of the Jefferson County Historical Society.

She has published pieces in local newspapers; in the *Mayflower Quarterly*, and an international publication; and is a contributor to *The Watershed Journal*, a local literary publication.

Myers served her community as president of the Ridgway Area School Board, president of the Elk County General Hospital Auxiliary and president of the Elk County Recreation and Tourist Council. She served on the GSMD 2014 Congress Planning Committee, researched and compiled *Junior Mayflower Descendants* booklets for the GSMD Juniors Program, was a chairperson of the GSMD Marketing Committee and served as membership chair and assistant to the Historian for the Society of Mayflower Descendants in Pennsylvania. She was regent of the DuBois-Susquehanna chapter of the Daughters of the American Revolution.

She is married to her high school sweetheart, John, and they are the parents of one son and have two grandsons.